Praise for **BLACK MAGIC**

"Chad has the unique ability to turn his experiences and the experiences of others into a guidebook that will inspire many healthy discussions. This is Chad's superpower."

—Morgan Freeman, actor

"Daring, urgent, and transformative. Not only did the stories and interviews in *Black Magic* forever change how I think about leadership and culture, they challenged me as a parent, friend, and citizen. This book will be required reading in our organization."

—Brené Brown, *New York Times* bestselling author of *Dare to Lead*

"It's a really incredible story. . . . I want everyone to read *Black Magic*."

—Dax Shepard, *The Armchair Expert*

"I greatly enjoyed *Black Magic*. I found it to be, at once, pulverizing, educational, and inspirational in a way that feels accessible. You should read this book."

—Shea Serrano, *#1 New York Times* bestselling author

"Thought-provoking and useful . . . Above all, *Black Magic* is an expression of an exciting and much-needed philosophy, and readers may be encouraged to mine gold from their own tough experiences."

—*The Washington Post*

"Readers will be moved most by how Sanders and his interviewees don't shy away from the pain of the discrimination they've endured, instead transforming suffering into a source of assurance and hope. The overarching vision here is one of making room for Blackness in every sphere and ensuring that being Black is not a detraction but rather a strength."

—*Booklist* (starred review)

"An engaging record of how Black pain and endurance can lead to Black excellence."

—*Kirkus Reviews*

"This inspirational account offers useful lessons on how 'power can be derived from trauma and suffering.'"

—*Publishers Weekly*

"*Black Magic* is the book we need urgently in this moment. Chad's voice is clear, direct, and honest. There is so much for us all to learn from the lives explored in this beautiful read."

—Angie Martinez, *New York Times* bestselling author, Grammy-nominated artist, and "The Voice of New York"

"Our world has never been more at peril, our country never more divided, and the need for smart, unifying voices never more clear. Chad's perspective is bold and unapologetic while simultaneously being inclusive and nonjudgmental. An incredibly difficult balance that *Black Magic* achieves marvelously."

—Will Packer, film and TV producer

"*Black Magic* is real. Chad Sanders takes us on a journey to unlock its secret with life stories that offer proof."

—Tom Straw, Emmy-nominated TV producer and #1 *New York Times* bestselling author

"An astonishingly original book! Chad Sanders makes a compelling case for the magic to be found in leveraging your authentic self in a business world that emphasizes conformity."

—Cal Newport, *New York Times* bestselling author of *Digital Minimalism* and *Deep Work*

"Chad's analysis of Black achievement is compelling and inspiring. In times like these, we need this book. Every human should read it."

—Pinky Cole, CEO and founder of Slutty Vegan, Atlanta

What Black Leaders Learned from Trauma and Triumph

BLACK MAGIC

CHAD SANDERS

Simon & Schuster Paperbacks
New York London Toronto Sydney New Delhi

Simon & Schuster Paperbacks
An Imprint of Simon & Schuster, Inc.
1230 Avenue of the Americas
New York, NY 10020

Some names and identifying details have been changed.
Some conversations have been reconstructed.

First Simon & Schuster trade paperback edition February 2022

For information about special discounts for bulk
purchases, please contact Simon & Schuster Special Sales at
1-866-506-1949 or business@simonandschuster.com.

The Simon & Schuster Speakers Bureau can bring authors to
your live event. For more information or to book an event, contact
the Simon & Schuster Speakers Bureau at 1-866-248-3049
or visit our website at www.simonspeakers.com.

Interior design by Lewelin Polanco

Manufactured in the United States of America

1   3   5   7   9   10   8   6   4   2

Library of Congress Cataloging-in-Publication Data is available.

ISBN 978-1-9821-0422-1
ISBN 978-1-9821-0423-8 (pbk)
ISBN 978-1-9821-0424-5 (ebook)

Dedication

For every wandering, Black dreamer. I am you.

For my parents, Monice and Bruce. Thank you for everything you poured into every single day. You showed us the importance of family, sacrifice, and independent thinking. I love you.

For my sister, Shannon. Thank you for teaching me how to read and write. But more, thank you for showing me how to create. I love you.

For my nephew, Fox. Thank you for inspiring me. I pray that you and your biggest dreams find each other. I love you.

For Juliana. Thank you for being creative. Thank you for being real. Thank you for being free. I admire you. I love you.

For Granna. Thank you for your kindness and wisdom. Thank you for Sweet Ginger. I love you.

For Aunt Susan. Thank you for your zen. Thank you for talking to me about bugs. I love you.

For my cousin, Trooper. Thank you for being a brother in every sense of the word. I love you.

For my cousin, Rachel. Thank you for being a sister in every sense of the word. I love you.

For Aunt Onita. Thank you for showing me artistry as a lifestyle. I love you.

For Uncle Butch. Thank you for your sense of humor. I love you.

For Aunt Pam. Thank you for community. I love you.

For the spirits of Grandma Maggie, Granddaddy O'Neal, Grandad Hodges, Aunt Sandra, Alicia, and Young June. For the spirits of every Black person gone too soon. Please watch over me.

Contents

Chapter Two
GRADE SCHOOL:
GIFTED AND TALENTED PROGRAMS,
PRIVATE SCHOOL, AND SEPARATION

Jewel Burks Solomon: "I had a conversation with a Black investor and he said, 'You're not going to be able to raise money with the team that you have currently.' He was like, 'You just can't. It's not gonna happen. You need to find a white man to do this with you.' "

Brian Shields: "I didn't fully realize what being 'Black' meant until one of my teachers in the third grade pulled me aside to make sure the other kids weren't taking advantage of me because I was the smart kid in class and the only Black kid in class."

DeRay McKesson: "I want Black people to understand that Blackness is its own sort of power and it's not only important in reference to other things. Our power does not lie solely in the fact that we've overcome trauma. Our power lies in the fact that we created in the midst of trauma."

Chapter Three
COLLEGE: HBCUS,
PWIS, AND HIGHER LEARNING

Grayson Brown: "I thought that I, as a human, could transcend racial dynamics. That is really dangerous, because eventually something happens that snaps you back and white people show you very clearly, and often quite damagingly to your person, that you're not the same."

Introduction

I remember the day I realized I couldn't play a white guy as well as a white guy. It felt like a death sentence for my career. I was twenty-three and working at Google in lily-white Silicon Valley. I was wearing a blue-checkered button-up shirt and khakis.

All my life I'd been told by white teachers in mostly white classrooms that my worth would be determined by my hard work and dedication. But as a Black boy, then a Black man, my experience outside those classrooms spoke more acutely: Whiteness outweighed hard work and dedication, as well as merit, potential, and vision, in a corporate environment. Whiteness was its own form of prestige trumping all skill sets and accolades.

If I wanted to be successful, I'd have to learn to emulate and genuflect to whiteness.

I had just left the safety of Morehouse College. For those four years at Morehouse, I never had to clench my teeth while an overzealous bro shouted "nigga" over rap lyrics or walk out of a classroom when a ham-fisted teacher explained the Middle Passage as an "unfortunate but economically efficient way of transporting cargo." No, those were high school problems for me. And they are dwarfed by the much more horrific problems of police violence, mass incarceration, crippling poverty, and the myriad systemic and incidental race crimes against Black people that occur daily. But it still sucked.

At Morehouse I felt safe and comforted in an environment where nearly everyone was Black. There were other forms of prejudice and competition that created hierarchy, like money, Greek organizations, and lingering skin-tone politics. But none of these loomed as ominously and constantly as race had in the mostly white classrooms where I was taught in grade school and then, later, in the mostly white offices where I stewed in the corporate world. At Morehouse and our sister school, Spelman, I was protected from the domineering nature of whiteness in a way that allowed me to stretch into my identity and find my own voice and ways of thinking. For the first time, I felt safe from judgments and microaggressions that seemed to lurk in every conversation outside those walls.

I believed that safety and comfort in my own skin would travel with me after college. I had context now. I knew my place in the universe and would not be shaken.

I was wrong.

I landed at Google with a thud. It was my first job. I understood my gig. I was organized and methodical enough to execute my duties as an associate in the company's lower rungs. But I felt like a cog in a corporate machine. I was bored and unsatisfied and desperately seeking purpose. I wanted to move up fast. I wanted to be seen. I wanted to be celebrated.

I observed that the fastest climbers, or even those just able to avoid the company's swift ax for underperforming talent, found their advantages socially. The climbers formed relationships with decision makers on a personal level. Every meeting, team offsite, and dinner was full of white colloquialisms and privileged talk—of international travel or some folk concert in San Francisco coming up that weekend. Company culture was a constant celebration of whiteness from my perspective. One's ability to join in on the party, whether authentic or contrived, at least partially determined one's trajectory in the company. There quickly formed a divide between those who could and those who couldn't fit in that roughly overlaid the company's color lines. In my observation, those who couldn't were deemed "cultural misfits"—not "Googly" enough. I saw several of those people let go, some of whom were my close friends who had attended HBCUs (historically Black colleges and universities) like I had.

This was Google's culture, but it was not unique. In Google's 2019 Annual Diversity Report the company reported that only 3.3 percent of Google employees self-identified as Black.[*] That same year Facebook reported that 3.8 percent of their employees identified as African-American.[†] In 2019, JPMorgan Chase & Co., the largest bank in the nation with $2.7 trillion in assets, self-reported that only 4 percent of the company's executives and senior-level managers were Black.[‡] The technology and finance industries are most notorious for their

---

[*] Google Diversity Annual Report 2019, https://static.googleusercontent.com /media/diversity.google/en//static/pdf/Google_diversity_annual_report _2019.pdf.

[†] Facebook Diversity Report 2019, https://diversity.fb.com/read-report/.

[‡] JP Morgan Chase Company Website, https://about.jpmorganchase.com/ content/dam/jpmc/jpmorgan-chase-and-co/documents/workforce-com position-disclosure.pdf.

whitewashed cultures, but wherever you find capitalism and "prestige," you will find cultural exclusivity.

I was perceptive enough to recognize the premium placed on assimilation, but too naive to see that its returns were limited—and presented risk to my mental health and self-esteem. So I flailed, awkwardly trying to emulate whiteness. I changed my wardrobe. Hence the blue-checkered button-up shirt and khakis. I reached deep into my childhood memories to pull out a harmless and convivial bro-y cadence I'd crafted in a majority white public high school to survive in white classrooms. I showed up alone to parties to avoid intimidating white peers with the presence of my Black friends. I rushed to immerse myself in white culture. I listened to white music. I made up stories of extravagant family holidays to faraway places to fill in the blanks, trying to make up for the space between the white world and me. It was ugly. Judge me. I was twenty-three and trying to keep my job.

I got what I wanted. I was included, but it came at a cost. Once I was technically "in" the world of which I had so badly wanted to be a part, I was at the bottom of the totem pole. These were, after all, environments designed to value whiteness above everything else. I was lonely because I pushed away friends who I thought weren't allowed in the white world. I was more dejected than ever, both ashamed for having abandoned the most robust parts of my identity and constantly carrying the unbearable weight of imposter syndrome. My discomfort bore out in my work. I performed well below expectations I had for myself, distracted by trying to walk the tightrope of being Black enough to look myself in the mirror but white enough to be seen.

It was exhausting.

So I quit. Not my job—but the entire charade of trying to be someone else, a "culture fit." Holding up a mask of whiteness became too heavy a burden. It was stunting my growth professionally and personally. I wasn't being promoted or celebrated at work. And I had isolated from my own people.

With few other options, I resigned to being . . . myself. In meetings I reverted to methods I'd learned not in classrooms, but at the dinner table with family or the barbershop, concrete basketball courts, the Morehouse College cafeteria, and Black Baptist churches. My tone became unflinching, sometimes even brash. I called colleagues and clients out for condescending or manipulative behavior. I told the truth when I felt microaggressed, silenced, or othered in work environments because of my race.

And my work performance started to take off.

Clients and colleagues respected me and began to defer to me. I was exposed to the company's more exciting initiatives, like Google X and YouTube, by leaders looking for outside perspectives from strong voices. I was flown all over the US and Europe with big budgets to develop new projects and to represent the company in new markets. My evaluation ratings soared. Finally, I was seen. Finally, I was celebrated. But most importantly, I realized that I had everything I needed to forge my own path in business. I had it before I ever went to Silicon Valley. I had developed grit, savvy, and foresight by walking the tightrope of Blackness my entire life. Enduring a Black experience in America prepared me to fight boardroom battles and solve business problems. Once I realized how I could use the preparation from those experiences to benefit Google, I began to see how I could use those abilities for my own personal gain.

My manager wrote a glowing review of my work at the time. It was meant to be shared with her managerial colleagues to determine my performance score, but she shared it with me. I saved it as a reminder of the new spirit I'd found by shedding the grotesque layers of white assimilation I'd pulled close to hide my identity. I'll paraphrase here:

Chad has found a wave of confidence and clarity of thought, voice, and vision that is pushing his work forward. He has an ability to shape his tone adeptly to reach audiences—colleagues, managers, clients, or otherwise—in a way that makes them feel welcomed and challenged. Chad is picking his spots well, knowing where to be and what to do. His vision belies his newness to the company. He is almost unrecognizable to the restless, naive person who walked onto our team a year ago. Our clients and partners are drawn to him and they are quiet and deferential when he proposes a plan of action or solution to a common problem. Chad is making magic.

She was right. Shortly after that review, I left Google to join a tech startup as a partner. During my time there, I was sent to Berlin to launch our first European operations. I realized again—this time in a foreign city—that I could draw upon skills forged by my racial experience to pave a business path. I needed to process and respond to information quickly, as I once did when a student was stabbed to death just feet away from me in front of my high school. I had to read body language and code-switch, a term used to describe alternating vernaculars, as

I had so many times traveling between the mostly white suburb where I lived to visit relatives in Blacker areas. I had heightened emotional intelligence, crafted through learning to understand and empathize with the lifestyles and experiences of white classmates, that helped me negotiate with German venture capitalists. A few years later, Kaplan Inc., a giant education-services company, bought our company, which now included European relationships I had forged.

Today, I've changed careers entirely, emboldened by reclaiming my gifts forged by Blackness. In addition to the book you're reading right now, I'm a writer of TV series and movies for Hollywood studios and networks. I've collaborated with Spike Lee, Morgan Freeman, and Will Packer, and I've been featured in *Forbes* and *Variety*. My Black experience gave me tools and values—presence of mind, empathy, independent thinking, conviction, comfort in isolation, work ethic, resourcefulness, bravery, focus, leadership, perseverance, community, detachment, charisma, problem solving, and faith—to carve my path.

I believe that a Black experience—often traumatic and made more so by heinous historic and present-day crimes—provides a set of skills and tactics that can lead to victories in business, art, and science. If you can survive your Black experience, you have learned so much that is useful that cannot be taught or bought. I call this Black Magic.

But I'm young and unwise. My perspective is limited. I look to others who have seen more, done more, and overcome more, to test this theory. I want to know how they've applied their own skills from their Black experiences to create, explore, innovate, and capitalize.

Is Black Magic real or am I rationalizing? Am I using outliers of a cruel system to feel hopeful? Am I reaching?

This book introduces successful Black businesspeople, artists, entertainers, scientists, and activists to explore the concept of Black Magic. They will share what they have learned, and how they used it to advance in a complex and conniving system. They spoke to me so that others may learn from their paths; so that young Black people who feel stuck will look inward and find what they need to succeed, amass wealth, and inspire the next generation.

If you can navigate Blackness, you can thrive in any high-stakes environment. If.

How to Read This Book

This book is an exploration of Black Magic—the tactics, skills, and habits Black leaders learned from traumatic and triumphant Black experiences.

Each section explores the spaces we inhabit as we learn, often treacherously, how to use our Black Magic. Each chapter is composed of interviews with Black leaders across industries and disciplines, with a focus on how their racial enduring forged or refined abilities that empowered them to succeed.

In the research process for this book I spoke to over two hundred Black people who inspire me. Some were world famous, others had no public profile at all. The interview subjects you'll find here are people who I knew well enough for them to share intimate and painful details from their lives. They were also those willing to share on record and risk offending neighbors, bosses, and people who buy their products or services. Most celebrities were not willing to take such risks, and thus you will probably not know the names of most of the interview subjects in this book, but their stories will move you.

The subjects were high achievers spanning diverse upbringings. They grew up all over the United States, in widely varying socioeconomic backgrounds. Some finished high school, some attended college, a few have higher degrees. They each see the world from a unique vantage point, and there are many areas where the subjects contradict one another. Their responses were only revised for grammar and syntax.

Do not expect to find in these pages an exact road map for success as a Black person. Expect instead to find the beginnings of a new science—not newly practiced, but newly labeled— within which you as the reader are welcome to explore, experiment, hypothesize, utilize, celebrate, criticize, respond, or dismiss altogether.

The core tenet of *Black Magic* is that power can be derived from trauma and suffering. I use the term "trauma" according to its precise definition: a deeply distressing or disturbing experience. Blackness is at times just that. Who would deny it?

As I write these words in 2020, Breonna Taylor and George Floyd recently became two casualties on the uncountable list of Black folks seemingly killed for being Black in the past four centuries. And as we watch, we brace for their killers to walk free, as history has shown us repeatedly; some of us mourn, fewer protest, and many more will push down the fear, anger, and sadness to face colleagues and bosses at work another day. However we respond in action, we all will carry the trauma of seeing images, learning of acquittals, and living with the memory of injustice that reinforce the message that our lives are not protected or valued. There is no silver lining to that trauma and no Black privilege that comes with it. You will find no argument in this book that Black people are at some imperceptible advantage because of suffering.

No. Racism sucks and it's literally killing us.

No one should have to endure trauma, but this is the state of the world for now. To have a chance at joy and peace, we have to study the design of this dangerous labyrinth. We have to understand what we're dealing with to get through it. There is information to be gleaned from facing and trying to survive racism. That information, collected through trauma, informs a set of tools and tactics that can be applied in other complex systems—such as school, business, entertainment, science, and religion. Those tools are what brilliant Black leaders have bravely shared in this book.

If your response to this premise is to say, "Well, I'm not Black but I've experienced trauma. What about me?" keep reading. You too possess a set of special tools.

For anyone who's never endured hardship, congratulations. Please find a seat in the back and be quiet.

For all others, welcome.

Chapter One

HOME AND NEIGHBORHOOD

"In 1944 a sixteen-year-old Black student in Columbus, Ohio, won an essay contest on the theme 'What to Do with Hitler after the War' by submitting the single sentence, 'Put him in a Black skin and let him live the rest of his life in America.'"

—Matthew Frye Jacobson, *Whiteness of a Different Color: European Immigrants and the Alchemy of Race*

I don't remember what I was wearing when I ran from my 250-square-foot apartment to Google's mammoth Chelsea office, which took up an entire city block.

I probably had on cargo shorts to survive New York's sweltering summer heat. Or maybe I wore them to look "Googly" in the office. I can't say.

But I remember clearly stepping into the building and staring down the cold, sterile corridor at the elevators. My brain was paralyzed. I wanted to turn and run out and hide under the covers and call my friends and scroll the horrifying words and images on Black Twitter. Even that seemed better than what I would do instead: shuffle along, into and up the elevator to the fifteenth floor, where I'd be greeted by my oblivious colleagues with a shit-eating grin on my face.

The night before, George Zimmerman had been ruled not guilty of second-degree murder in the shooting death of seventeen-year-old Trayvon Martin, and I was not okay. I was full of grief and fear.

I did not feel Googly.

If my coworkers cared or could tell I was in pain, they didn't show it. And I did just enough to make sure they couldn't sense my anguish. I trudged through a micro-kitchen stocked with Greek yogurts and organic snacks to my cubicle. I asked my colleagues about significant others and babies and dogs who were all very important to them. They were as willing as ever to filibuster about these characters in their lives. A couple asked how I was doing. I knew the question was an empty gesture.

Good. Great. I'm fine. Whatever will check the box that we were done and let me get to my seat.

It seemed inhumane that I was expected to show up at work and send emails like any other day. I had seen the photos of Trayvon. That kid looked just like me. I wondered how my coworkers could look at me and not see him. But perhaps they couldn't really see him and they couldn't really see me.

Well, one of them could see me—Andrea Taylor. Dre was Stanford-educated, and light enough to pass for white, but she chose not to. She emerged at my cubicle with her hair in a big, curly bun.

"Come on, let's go," she said. I followed her.

Dre led me into an overly lit meeting room. She touched my hand, lightly.

"Chad, I can tell you're not okay," she said.

How could she tell if nobody else could? I'm almost sure I didn't cry, because my mom had taught me since I was ten years old that Black folks weren't allowed to cry at work.

The fear of death was on me. I thought I was hiding it well, but Andrea could smell it in a way none of my white colleagues could or cared to. Their apathy felt personal. Andrea's comforting presence reassured me I was not alone, but icy loneliness was otherwise a common feeling for me in certain corporate environments.

Andrea sat there beside me, holding on to my arm. Maybe I yelled, maybe I just sat there. I really don't remember. She knew why I was hurting but she let me tell her anyway. It wasn't that an innocent kid was dead. It wasn't that his killer was acquitted. I'd known as long as I'd known anything to expect such atrocities from this country, our home. That was on brand.

What hurt me was that I was expected to smile and drone and punch out mind-numbing emails and laugh at my coworkers' corny jokes and affirm their experiences without receiving affirmation in return. I knew what Andrea was about to say. She was hurting too, but she processed the pain much more stoically. She gave me three minutes to be emotional. And then . . .

"Okay, Chad," she said. "C'mon, we have to get back to work."

I knew she was right. As two of the very few young Black people at Google, we both felt immense pressure to perform at the highest level. I couldn't risk squandering my opportunity because of feelings. If I did, would the same opportunity be available for someone like me next year? Would I be able to support myself? The cost of trading time at my desk for time in the conference room, sorting myself, was too expensive.

And for those few minutes I spent in the conference room, I wanted to apologize to my father.

My dad is a tough guy. He's a college athlete. He's a lawyer. He was born in Detroit, in the 1950s. Growing up, he shared a bed with his older brother in the kitchen. His father was an army veteran with a sixth-grade education. During the 1967 Detroit riot, one of the deadliest in American history, my dad sat with his father in front of Grandaddy O'Neal's small laundromat bearing shotguns in case the mostly Black rioters didn't notice or care that their business was Black-owned.

When I was six years old my family moved up-county, from a small townhouse on the Maryland side of the D.C. border to a quaint cul-de-sac, and this, I think, made my dad keep a very close eye on my sister and me as well as our white neighbors.

We moved from a modestly sized brick townhouse to a single-family house with a two-car-garage. Our old neighborhood was diverse, with a number of Black and Latinx families. Our new neighborhood was mostly white. Our old neighbors were an eclectic mix of government employees, teachers, and laborers. Our new neighbors were more affluent white-collar professionals. We had *moved on up*. With its square lawns, tall trees, and general American Dream–iness, our new neighborhood resembled the gated community where Trayvon was murdered for being Black after the streetlights came on.

But what I saw, as a child, was a giant playground. I was six, the age where I wanted to explore on my own. I thought I would ride my tricycle down our street or trudge through backyards adjacent to ours, as freely as the white kids in our neighborhood did. My father knew better. Like Andrea at Google, he knew there was a different set of rules for me.

My dad was a hands-on father. Not in the physical sense—in fact I can't remember ever being spanked by him. But he paid close and constant attention to my every movement. He coached my youth basketball games and was particularly firm with me compared to the other players' parents. After every game and every practice from age six through fourteen, he would run through a list of detailed questions about specific plays and decisions I made. These intense discussions often felt like emotional interrogations.

But if I tried to slither out of the questions for a bathroom break, or hide behind my mother, he was always there, on the other side, waiting with fixed intention.

"Why didn't you shoot the ball more? What did you see when you made this decision? Why are you passing the ball to James so much? Do you think he's a better shooter than you?" he would say, plowing through one question to the next before I could answer.

Every discussion was followed by another—a meta-discussion on how basketball principles we explored related to life decisions.

"Every shot you pass up is a missed opportunity, Chad. What do you think happens to Black boys who grow up passing on opportunities in this world?" he asked.

It all felt very urgent. Everything felt urgent.

He approached my schoolwork with the same hovering fervor. We'd sit side by side at the dining room table every night, mowing through hours of homework, studying for tests, arguing, struggling, learning together. The white neighborhood kids would show up at the door and ring the bell to see if I could come out and play.

My dad would crack the door just enough for them to see

me sitting there in front of a table covered in books and scattered papers. The white neighborhood kids would ask my dad if I could join them outside, and he'd quickly, gruffly, inform them that I was unavailable. Slam. Click. He'd shut the door, shaking the bottom two levels of our three-story house, then snap the lock closed. He wanted them, and me, to get the message that I would not be joining them anytime soon. Perhaps never, if that's how long it took for me to finish my homework. At times, I felt trapped.

But I had my father in my house. Many of my Black friends didn't.

As I grew, my high school coach took over my basketball training. Coach Pigrom was only thirty, a Black man who had played college ball at HBCU Hampton University. He was even more no-nonsense than my dad, but still my father hovered and pressed. He'd watch my basketball practices from the gymnasium window. He was the only dad who did that. When my teammates and I lined up on the baseline of the basketball court for sprints, a few would make jokes about my dad, who was always there watching. I was embarrassed, but I guessed that underneath their jokes was harmless envy. They loved to spend time hanging around my dad, maybe as a proxy for their own.

We'd pile into his Acura SUV on weekends and he'd drive us across the county to high school football games, teenage dance clubs, parties, and fairs. Five, six, seven of us Black teenagers would fold into the back of his car and rap along to Kanye West's *College Dropout* album, which had just come out, or my dad's favorite, Tupac. When we arrived at any destination, my dad would usually go inside to inspect the premises then sit out in the parking lot, watching the door.

I'd try to push him out of his watching. I wanted to assert myself as a man I'd yet become, and to me that meant I needed to get out from under my father's supervision. Sometimes I'd sneak around after curfew to see girlfriends or go to parties. As I grew, I wondered what or who my dad was always on the lookout for. I'd find that out later.

When I turned fifteen, my dad realized that he couldn't be everywhere I was, so he laid out very clear rules for my conduct in our upper-middle-class neighborhood.

- Always protect your freedom.
- No hats, du rags, or headwear of any kind in the car.
- Drive below the speed limit. If you get pulled over, put your hands where the police can see them. Don't make hard eye contact with the officer. Address the officer respectfully as sir.
- You can play with white kids in the neighborhood, but don't go in their houses.
- Don't get your sense of self-worth from depictions of Black people in the news, popular music, or popular movies and television. They will destroy you.
- Avoid interactions with the police.

I bristled at these rules, but I followed them, like all the rules that came before. My dad never really yelled at me off the basketball court. He never had to. I knew that he wanted to protect me. I don't know how I knew, but I just knew.

When I was in middle school, maybe twice a year, my dad would follow my school bus as it weaved between white neighborhoods picking up "Gifted and Talented" kids to take cross-county to our public school. The shrewdest preteens recognized I was insecure about being a Black kid who lived in a nice neighborhood with attentive parents, because that way of being ran counter to stereotypes. So they needled me when they saw me sweating over my dad's "overprotective" hawking eye.

"Hey dude, isn't that your *dad*? What's he doing?" one of the white kids would always ask, loud enough to catch the other kids' attention—and shame me. I'd shrink lower into one of the green leather seats of those big yellow buses and clutch my black JanSport backpack. I'd pull out my three-ring binder and busy myself with extra credit math problems to take my mind off of my humiliation. Then I'd peek around the side of one of those big stiff seats, out of the bus's wide back window and we'd make quick eye contact, my dad and I. I'd sneer. He would just smile back at me.

This one time, Trevor Willock, the *cool* kid with slicked hair whose father had divorced and married much younger, blurted out:

"Does your dad think the bus driver's gonna forget where our school is? What the hell is he doing back there?"

The coolest among us had started cursing by then. I wish I'd known the answer to his question. I do now. If I could go back, I'd give my twelve-year-old self the answer so he could spit it at Trevor.

"He's protecting me, Trevor. From being Emmett Till or Trayvon Martin or some other little memorialized Black boy. He's protecting me for as long as he possibly can, before it's out of his control," I'd have said. Instead, that day, I just squirmed deeper into the green leather seat.

I'm not sure if my dad clocked all my eye-rolling and sighing back then, but I know for certain he ignored me if he did. He was determined to fulfill the most important duty of fatherhood. He was on a mission to keep his Black son alive.

The danger my dad was always defending against came in many forms, some of them confusing. It could be a white woman walking her dog off leash in the park; it could be a racist neighbor overzealously playing out his American hero fantasies with a gun; it could be a cop who woke up on the wrong side of the bed. Whatever the danger, my dad was committed to keeping me under his supervision until I was mature enough and savvy enough to protect myself.

My father protected me by enforcing an elaborate set of rules. A decade later in a Google conference room, Andrea did the same thing, in her own way. She knew that what I needed, even if just for a few minutes, was to be seen. I needed for a moment to have my humanity affirmed. I needed to be with another Black person who understood the emotions boiling inside me; to nod and give me permission to be broken for a moment. And then I needed her to look me in the eye and tell me to get back to work. She provided me the safety to cry at work, but only for a moment in private. Because she knew, like my dad, that regardless of my feelings, my fears, and the danger I faced every day, that I needed to get back to that desk and do my job just like I needed to get on that bus every day and go to school and learn. Because my life and my livelihood depended on it, as well as the life and livelihood of the next Black person to come after me.

◆ ◆

While my father seemed to focus on rules that maintained my family's physical safety, my mother pushed my sister and me to strategize and achieve. This was her way of giving us financial safety. She taught us the importance of education, corporate advancement, and earning as ways for us as Black people to protect ourselves down the line from misinformation, financial predators, and unexpected disasters. The four of us—mom, dad, sister, brother—sat down for dinner as a family nearly every weeknight in that three-story house on the cul-de-sac. My parents took turns cooking while my sister and I set the table and listened to Stevie Wonder playing in the background. My late maternal grandfather's paintings adorned the yellow walls of the kitchen. He was a lieutenant colonel in the army and a Vietnam veteran. His paintings depicted people alone with nature. A bullfighter awaiting a charging bull. A camper alone beside a bonfire at night in the woods.

The television was always off. My Xbox was unplugged for the night so I wouldn't try to rush through a meal to get back to it. A ringing house phone went unanswered. Door-to-door salespeople stopped coming at dinnertime, because my father warded them off. Before an unsuspecting Jehovah's Witness or Cutco knife salesman could even open his mouth, my dad would make waste of him.

"We don't want any and if you keep coming back here it's going to be a problem," he said before the guy got a word of his spiel out.

My parents protected dinnertime because it was their chance to listen to us, and to teach us who we were and where we came from, before the outside world could force its Eurocentric perspective into our developing minds. And that sort of enrichment required a high level of insulation and focus from all four of us. No distractions.

My mom was an executive at Verizon for most of my childhood, and she ran our kitchen like her boardroom. Dinnertime was regimented. Each time we sat down at our rectangular wooden table, we'd first say grace together. We took turns speaking to God on the family's behalf at each sitting. Then, my mom would recount the activities of the day at her Fortune 500 employer. By twelve I was familiar with rebrands, layoffs, mergers and acquisitions, initial public offerings, stock options, office politics, and the unstated rules of corporate culture. My mom engaged us in these conversations not as children, but as thought partners. We were invested spectators as she ascended the ranks from entry-level MBA to senior director over the course of my childhood. Race was an important factor in every discussion.

She'd ask what my sister and I thought she should tell her white male boss about her white female subordinate who'd been undermining her for weeks. She considered our thoughts and feedback carefully. I was eleven, my sister fourteen.

We'd brainstorm together with my father until we found a solution we could all live with. We were a mini war room. My mom often reminded us that business was a game, with rules, and additional nuance and risk for Black people. But like any game, it could be solved, and won. I found over time that living as a Black person is a game of its own, with the highest stakes and a similar set of rules.

In high school, I began to jot down the rules in business that I learned at our dinner table boardroom. I've paraphrased some of them here:

- Money controls all important decisions. The closer you sit to the money, the more valuable and safe you will be as an employee.
- Someone, somewhere is accounting for you as a human with a dollar amount attached to your name. That is your capitalist value. Your leverage (or lack thereof) can be reduced to that dollar amount. Be aware of it.
- In hard times, company culture craters. The leverage created by the money you make the company and the strength of your relationships is your safety net.
- In good times for a company, opportunities for promotions and growth emerge, and the money you make the company and the strength of your relationships are your leverage to access them.
- Always make your boss look good to her boss and make sure your boss knows you've done so.
- Value is measured by outcomes and not process. No points awarded for trying hard. No bonuses for sending the most emails.
- Do your job first before helping others to do theirs. You will never be rewarded in a way that feels adequate for helping other people do their jobs, especially if that aid comes at the expense of your job. Do your job.
- If you report an issue about a colleague to Human Resources, know that two people will thereafter be examined closely and considered potential threats to the business: the person you reported and you.
- Don't cry at work. Don't do it.

ED BAILEY

"Call it what you want. I'm still here."

Ed is an executive coach for Silicon Valley leaders and an NFL agent and business consultant. He formerly led teams in Sales and HR as an executive at Google and LinkedIn and as a business management consultant at McKinsey & Company. He earned his MBA at Stanford GSB and his BS in Mathematics at Michigan State University.

When I started working at Google, the execs called Ed "Papa BOLD." He was a sales executive, but in his spare time he built Google's Building Opportunities for Leadership and Development program to help hundreds of Black and brown young adults get hired at Google. I was one of those kids.

I was walking through one of Google's main campus hallways when I first saw Ed. He stood out as a big Black man with broad shoulders and a full beard. Ed was giving an orientation talk to the new hires. The Google employees, mostly white, wore company-issued hats with silly pinwheels to announce their newness. Ed was more dignified, all six-foot-three of him, wearing a Chicago Cubs T-shirt and shorts.

The audience members were quiet and attentive, jotting notes as he spoke. Ed captivated those white people. I watched from the back row as he plowed through his lecture with no notes, holding his body upright with complete confidence. He owned the room. That struck me. And he spoke from his belly, not shrinking his body or raising the pitch of his voice to make himself unthreatening.

When a tall, square-jawed blond man in the front row tried to interrupt Ed's spiel with a question, Ed drove straight through the man's interruption without skipping a beat. Ed gave the man a wink to let him know he clocked him and that he'd get back to him after he'd finished his train of thought.

I knew so little as a twenty-two-year-old working for the first time in a large company, but I learned quickly that to excel I'd have to get white people to listen to me. I thought that to get their attention, I'd have to emulate them. I thought I should dress as they did and talk as they did and shrink in moments when they didn't want me around. I call that process of changing to appease white people "racial duality." I showed up as a "whiter" version of myself when I thought it would save me. Many Black people feel forced to adopt this process, this reality of dual selves, to be palatable and included, especially in corporate worlds.

When I interviewed Ed, I wanted to understand how he commanded the respect of white people as a big, Black man from the hood. I wanted to explore Ed's ability to connect with white people in a way that seemed so effortless. I wanted to learn from his mastery of racial duality.

I thought mastering racial duality was a form of Black Magic, an ability that could help Black people manipulate situations. But Ed finds racial duality to be a painful burden—one he'd had to carry since he was a kid, to survive his old neighborhood. I was struck by Ed's conviction in his belief that Black people actually lose more than we gain by switching back and forth between personas to accommodate white people.

———

Chad: To start us off, can you run me through the geographic stops from your life dating back to childhood, and your focus in each one of those stops?

Ed: So geographically speaking from zero to eighteen I was in Chicago, I grew up in one house my entire time there, on the West Side of the city in the midst of a neighborhood where a lot of gangs and gang leadership resided but it looked okay from the outside. In other words there were lots of houses and bungalows and stuff but the freaks really came out at night.

From eighteen to twenty-two I was at Michigan State. In between there I spent a summer in Minneapolis and I spent a summer in this town called Lodi, California, which is a wine manufacturing town. The big employer there was the General Mills plant, which is why I was there. From twenty-two to twenty-four I lived in downtown Chicago, where I was working at McKinsey. And then twenty-four to twenty-six I was at Stanford at the GSB, but I was one of the few folks that lived off campus both years. From twenty-six to thirty-four I basically lived in Los Altos, that comprised both my Google era and my LinkedIn era. And then I got my place in Sacramento when I was thirty-four and I've been here in the Bay Area ever since.

Chad: What was your purpose at each one of those stops? And what was your relationship to your race?

Ed: Both my mom and my dad grew up in families with at least five kids that were very poor. So both of my parents were first-generation projects. My mom lived in a condemned house, my dad lived in some of the worst projects in Chicago his entire life. So resources were never plentiful for them and they didn't really care about that kind of stuff. In addition, both families were Jehovah's Witnesses, so there was a level of separatism there and both my parents really didn't get along with their mothers as they became adults.

All of that led to a scenario where my parents moved to a nicer part of the west side and basically away from everything they grew up around. So I was always different as a child from the rest of my family. I was different from cousins, aunts, uncles, and stuff on both sides because of that distance. I was different both in terms of philosophical distance as well as actual distance, because my mom and dad both had cars but no one else in the family had vehicles. So we could get to them, but they couldn't get to us. So my experience outside of school was just me, my mom, and my dad. And then when my brother was born he was added to that.

There was always a challenge for me to connect to my family members and cousins. They were having conversations about common experiences and then I would drop into their environment and I couldn't relate. I didn't play with the toys because my parents believed toys were distractions. I didn't watch the TV shows or listen to the music they listened to, so there was no connection there. I had to learn at an early age how to be in an environment and connect while not being connected.

Chad: How did that translate once you started school?

Ed: Up to eighth grade, I was part of a gifted and talented program, so I didn't go to the neighborhood schools. I might see the neighborhood kids for an hour or two on weekends, but I was separate from them too. That led to something my dad and I always talk about: neighborhood rules. I wasn't allowed to talk to the neighborhood kids about how smart I was. I wasn't allowed to talk about what kind of stuff my family had in the house. I wasn't allowed to talk about the experiences I had because in my dad's perspective—and he was right about most of it—in the type of neighborhood we were in, people see that stuff and they try to take it.

My house was probably broken into every year for ten consecutive years, and I would see some of the neighborhood kids with the toys they stole. But yet, I had to figure out how to get along with them. That was an interesting experience, and particularly with guys, that led me to not build close relationships with men for a long, long time. There was no trust level there. I knew that for guys my age and a little older—call it eight to twenty years old—it was every man for himself and guys were trying to get anything they could at all costs. If they had to sell drugs or rob people and take stuff from others, even their friends, they would.

I could never trust the decision-making of the guys where I lived, so I'd never get in the car with them. I would rarely even walk places. Those became saving characteristics for me, because there were times where I chose not to go on a ride and the group in the car got shot up. When I explain this to people, some say that feels kind of separatist or kind of extreme, but it actually saved my life on multiple occasions. You can call it what you want. I'm still here.

Chad: Did those habits of separation follow you into the classroom?

Ed: When I got to school it was a non-Black world. There were white people, there were Hispanics, there were Asians, but basically all the smartest kids in that part of Chicago were in one school, and even among that group I was sort of extra-gifted with math and analytics. So on one hand I was a competitor with my classmates and on another hand I never got to spend any time with them because my parents didn't believe in me spending the night in other houses because of all the religious stuff. I wasn't going to birthday or Christmas parties or anything like that. So I had to learn to support people from a distance. I had to learn to show people that I knew something was important to them without having the ability to participate.

Those three major dualities forged my personality: separation from family, separation from neighborhood, and separation from my peers, at school and in social environments.

When I got to Michigan State, I was really excited about being able to be friends with people of color on my level academically. But I quickly realized many of the other students of color weren't nearly as prepared to be successful. Many of them lacked fundamental tools to be successful there. I spent a lot of time helping them, tutoring them, coaching them to make sure they got through classes so they could stay at school and so I could have friends. I lost three or four close friends over the first couple years because they just couldn't hack it academically. As I took on leadership responsibilities at the dorm and on campus, I had to stay grounded so I could still be one of the crew. I had to make sure I wasn't automatically alpha. I had to learn how to lead when it wasn't what I wanted to do but it was necessary for the best outcome. I had to learn to lead my friends in structured environments and then just be one of the people in unstructured environments, and I had to learn to identify the difference between the two types of environments.

On the flip side, I still had to find ways to relate to my honors college folks and scholarship folks who weren't Black. So when I decided we were going to put on a Kwanzaa celebration for the first time in Michigan State's history, a lot of my fellow scholarship kids were like "Why are you doing that? Why are you trying to accentuate Blackness so much? Is there a problem?"

Later, when Student Body president elections came up, all the candidates were white males and they were searching for someone to just diversify the ballot. My name came up. I had already agreed to enter the pool of candidates before I realized *why* my name came up. But when I found out they just needed someone of color on the ballot, I felt like I *needed to win*. I thought I needed to win so people's behaviors and thoughts would change. The feeling came from things I experienced when I was younger. I thought *Yeah, I might be an outsider for things beyond my control, but don't discount my abilities based on that. And don't think that because I spend a lot of time on the brown side of campus that I don't have the white credentials and capabilities.*

I won the election by connecting with students who felt disenfranchised, and it led to one of the biggest learning experiences of my life. I learned what happens when you achieve something that you don't really want or care about. To boil it down, you end up not doing as well and making yourself look bad in different ways. You end up going through heartache because you fight what you can't do versus what you want to do when they don't line up. And I think that is a big downside of having to go through racial duality. You end up in situations when you have to choose between solidifying or debunking the world's view of you or solidifying or debunking your own version of yourself. That leads to what I call "Ghost Chasing" or this internal struggle between which person is real. You end up with multiple personas, and it gets difficult to manage them after a while.

Chad: What does that look like?

Ed: In college I did an internship for two years with General Mills. Loved it. Very diverse company. Learned a lot. Had a lot of support multiculturally. I was excited about pursuing that opportunity as a place to work after college. I felt comfortable there. Then this magical thing that I knew nothing about called McKinsey & Company dropped out of the sky and decided to interview at Michigan State for the first and last time over the course of a twenty-year period. Even though I knew General Mills was better for me, McKinsey was more prestigious. And so I did what I did with the student body president election. I made sure I killed it and I got the offer.

Even though all my friends were going back to General Mills and I knew I would have a support system there and I knew I would be in a place where I could be happy at work, I chose to do the shiny thing by going to work at McKinsey because as a Black person, sometimes to get ahead and get opportunities, you have to do the shiny thing.

Chad: Why? What does it cost you if you don't choose the shiny thing? What does it cost you when you do choose the shiny thing?

Ed: First, when you're in what I'll call *high achievement environments*, there's always the recognition, implicitly or explicitly, that there have been very few if any people of color who have done what you're doing. If you're at all sensitive to the outside world, you realize you're not just representing you. There's something on the front of the jersey that you wear that becomes more important than who you actually are and what you care about. And that's why I think, in many cases, pursuing the shiny, known, visible opportunity, even if it's not best for you or what you want, becomes an important decision for Black people.

What does it cost you when you *don't* pursue the shiny thing? Well, I think what it costs you is the opportunity to learn what other parts of the world look like, and to go into places you wouldn't have had access to otherwise. And to learn from people, learn from circumstance, learn emotionally how to deal with all of it. And more importantly, if you don't do the shiny thing, it can cost other people like you the same opportunity in the future. Oftentimes, in those environments, you're the gatekeeper's first chance to experience a Black person who has the capabilities that you have. And the gatekeeper's experience with you is going to define whether or not they're open to more experiences like that for people like you. So shoving what they believe to be a gift back in their faces can be unhealthy. It can lead to doors closing for many more deserving, better fitting Black people who come behind you.

But the cost of pursuing shiny objects is twofold as well. For one, as a person, you can waste your time pursuing things that aren't for you and suffer emotional pain when those things don't go well. Even if they do go well, you know that you aren't doing what you're meant to do and you can't enjoy life the same way. For me, that was particularly painful because I've always had a really good sense of what I wanted to do in my life, and the McKinsey choice led to a bunch of decisions that I made that weren't in the best interest of my personal happiness. Instead I continued to pursue exploring and entering slightly forbidden worlds to learn for the sake of advancing Black people.

Take my experience working at McKinsey for example. After undergrad, I made this decision to go to McKinsey and I didn't know what the hell McKinsey was. I knew they helped other companies do stuff, which to be honest, where I'm from, didn't make much sense to me. But everyone said it was the hardest company to get into and the best company to work at, so I went. And, boy, was the world opened up to me. It exposed me to simple things. For instance, my family never went out to eat growing up, and I had never been to a nice restaurant before I worked at McKinsey. I had never been around wealthy people. I had never been around executives. I had read all the books and articles and stuff so I could have conversations, but it was just a really foreign environment. I had grown up opting out of foreign environments that weren't comfortable, for survival. This was the beginning of a period where I was starting to process the fact that what I actually had to do was opt into foreign environments in order to be successful. My comfort zone said hell no, but I knew that to trailblaze for my people I had to.

I learned a lot at McKinsey, but it wasn't very fun for me because I thought the work was really inefficient. There were times where I was sitting there waiting for someone else with more authority to allow me to do something that I may or may not have thought was useful. I didn't have much time to spend with anyone except my girlfriend because I was on the road all the time for the job. The money was great, but it didn't feel worth it at the end of the day. And most importantly, I never wanted to work there.

Chad: What was your relationship with whiteness at McKinsey?

Ed: I didn't really see it that way at McKinsey. If I look at my class of business analysts, there were twenty of us. There were three Black people in that class. I was the only Black male. And then there were seventeen white people. Thirteen of us were men and four were women. Within that group, we were just peers trying to survive McKinsey and there was no relationship with whiteness or Blackness or race or anything. We were just twenty young people trying to survive the madness that is working in a high-stakes business.

But my relationship to Blackness was interesting. McKinsey's Black network was called BCSS or Black Client Services Staff. Its origin was in Chicago. The first couple Black partners were from Chicago, and I worked in Chicago while I was at the company. Also, the most important person in any consulting firm—which is the person who does the assignment of analysts to projects—was also Black. And so, because of that, I had access to a power structure that gave me an opportunity to understand McKinsey in a way that was actually kind of unfair. It was the rare corporate environment where I had access to rare information as a Black person. That was really important for me in some pivotal moments. But it also underscored to me why it was so important that I made sure I did what I could to open doors for other people.

Chad: You said earlier that something problematic about duality is that you can end up with multiple personas. Did you feel that in your experience at McKinsey? Or did that develop elsewhere?

Ed: I actually didn't feel that at McKinsey. But the only reason I would say I didn't feel it is because McKinsey was life for those two years. There was no outside life. There was no other person I had to be. And so there wasn't as strong of a duality conflict—I just wasn't myself. I was just completely in another persona for those two years. And I think that had an impact on me. I was almost completely a character at that point.

Chad: Considering the path of your life—from grade school to college, McKinsey, Stanford, Google, Cisco, LinkedIn—the entire path. How would you quantify the percent of space in your brain occupied by managing the various personalities you needed to display at each stop?

Ed: That's a really good question and I was hoping you'd get to that. Middle school, I'd say 80 percent. High school, 40 percent. Undergraduate school at Michigan State, 60 percent. McKinsey, 95 percent. Stanford Graduate School of Business, 5 percent. Google, between 50 and 85 percent, depending on what I was doing. LinkedIn, 95 percent. Cisco was probably 50 percent. And now, 10 percent.

Chad: And what has it cost you to spend so much of your brainpower managing personalities within yourself?

Ed: Three years on the couch with my therapist twice a week. It cost me and several other people fun experiences because I was dealing with depression, social anxiety, PTSD, and the results of having to deal with all of that. It probably cost me two promotions at Google, one promotion at LinkedIn, and at least one promotion at Cisco.

Chad: You've made it clear that there were costs to your energy and mental health in managing dualities. What did you learn from that twenty-five-year process? Have you used or wielded any of that for success? Have you been able to fine-tune the muscles for your own advantage?

Ed: I think that because I spent a lot of time by myself, throughout my youth, I did develop a capability to think independently and to only be moved by better information and not by who it was coming from. And I think that is an advantage that plays out today and will play out in spades as my life continues to evolve. I think that I understood the importance of doing my own research and creating my own perspectives on things and fitting other people's information into that, versus starting with other people's information and then figuring out how much I could do with that until I have to start thinking for myself.

Chad: Do you feel like you have enough perspective and distance to opt in or out of duality?

Ed: My visceral answer is I think I've always tried to opt out of duality. I now have enough information to know why and when and how to exercise duality and to do that in a healthy way that's not self-destructive for me and other people. I always intellectually and emotionally knew the concept of duality was stupid and no one should have to go through that, but I also logically understood that in certain situations duality was unavoidable. But it took me a very long time to come to grips with exercising duality in a healthy way versus fighting and being willing to murder myself internally or externally to avoid it.

JASON CRAIN

"I recognized that white Kansas City and Black Kansas City were two totally fucking different things."

Jason is a tech and restaurant entrepreneur, startup advisor and investor, film producer, product owner at Amazon, real estate investor, and world traveler. He cofounded Partpic, a visual hardware recognition software, later acquired by Amazon. Before that, he was an executive at Google and Shazam. He is also chairman of the board for ScholarMade Achievement Place, a charter school in Little Rock, Arkansas, founded in 2018. Jason's achievements landed him a place in the 2016 *Forbes* 30 Under 30 manufacturing list. Jason earned his MBA at Kellogg School of Management and BAs in Marketing and Spanish at Morehouse College. That's where I met him.

Jason was the first of our friends to get rich, and he did it by building a company and selling it. In this interview, I was prepared to ask him about the process of raising money as a Black entrepreneur. I wanted to know the ways in which having money has affected his life. But Jason took control of the conversation and steered us to a more compelling topic: his experience growing up in his neighborhood in Kansas City. Jason highlighted two important experiences that made him a successful entrepreneur.

The first was the time he spent as a kid working with his father. The men on Jason's father's side of the family ran a nightclub in a rough part of Kansas City, where, as a teenager, Jason learned to run a business, from stocking the bar to counting the money in the register at the end of each night. It was hard work, but everyone worked hard. The second was the time he spent with his mother's family. His mom's side of the family faced constant struggles, including murder, poverty, and teen pregnancy. That gave Jason fuel and purpose to provide relief for himself and the people he loved. Jason stressed how both sides of his family influenced his outlook and shaped his success. Though some might see Jason's mom's side as a disadvantage, he never did. It drove him.

I admire Jason's perspective. One side of his family showed him how to provide a living; the other showed him the urgent and dire need to provide a living. Jason underscored that these experiences were the source of his Black Magic: he felt the need to provide resources, and learned the ethic to create them.

———

Jason: I'm Jason Crain, I am a Kansas City, Missouri, native. I currently live in Atlanta, Georgia, and I work for Amazon.com as an entrepreneur in residence and product manager. I've been in technology my entire career, starting at Google, then went to Shazam, then started my own tech startup in computer vision. We sold that startup to Amazon.com about eighteen months ago, and my responsibility now is leading data acquisition for our computer vision team and integrating our Partpic technology into Amazon's mobile app.

Chad: How did you grow up? What did your parents do for work? How were you raised?

Jason: I grew up modestly in Kansas City. I saw a lot, on both sides of the spectrum. My parents had me when they were in high school. My mother had me as a senior in high school at seventeen years old, and my father was just eighteen, and they didn't have much. My mother was one of seven kids. By the time she had me, all five other sisters and her one older brother already had multiple kids. So she grew up around young parents. My uncle, her brother, was murdered—shot and killed at a skating rink—so I never got to know him but I got to meet his kids in other cities.

On my mother's side, pretty much everyone is still living below the poverty line. They struggled with teenage pregnancy. They lived in not so good areas and had to fight the battles of living in Kansas City without having much.

On the other side, my father came from a divorced household, but a household that was grounded in Christianity and the Baptist faith. They didn't have a lot either but they lived a different life from my mother's family. My grandfather, who is the only person in my immediate family to have gone to college, took that college degree and was also an entrepreneur before me. He spent his whole life savings pursuing entrepreneurship, and to some degree you could consider it a failure, but he was able to create a life for my father. That life wasn't full of riches, but it was a life grounded in responsibility and working and doing whatever you gotta do to provide for your family.

My great-uncles on my father's side were also all entrepreneurs. They were fairly known in the Kansas City area because they owned a nightclub called Epicureon, which I now own with my father. That nightclub was a staple in the Black community. The club provided outlets for me and my brother to work from the time I was old enough to walk—whether it was just yard work at the club or stocking the bar in high school. My job was to make sure that the bar had liquor every night.

And I had a key and I was responsible for going in and filling the bar. My father's side of the family provided me with structure, foundation, and religion, and a focus on working and hustling and doing whatever you gotta do.

My mother's side of the family showed me struggle. Folks were in and out of jail, but that was the side I spent most of my time with. My mother had five sisters and two or three of them had at least five kids. So I had hella cousins. In elementary school I had cousins in every grade at my school. We ran the school.

So while I was being raised by my mother's side of the family, my father's side of the family provided that structure and guidance that made it possible for me to be successful.

Chad: You've built a career in the tech industry primarily. We worked together at Google, you were an equity owner at Shazam, and you cofounded Partpic. Now you're an entrepreneur in residence at Amazon. None of those places are filled with Black people. None of those places are even representative of the national demographics in terms of Black and brown people. You are a Black man under thirty-five from Kansas City with what you just described as a humble beginning. How have you been able to navigate those kinds of environments to plow your way to selling a company for millions of dollars and establishing yourself as a leader in technology?

Jason: I think it starts with what my family instilled in me, which was a need to provide. I saw how lack of access and resources impacted both sides of my family, but my father's side of the family was a shining example of an ability to push through and work through it regardless of the outcome. That determination and motivation is really the backbone of my success. Most times I didn't know what I was doing or know what the outcome of my actions would be. I was just doing what I thought I was supposed to do or what I was told I was supposed to do at each stage.

One of the things that changed my life was going to my high school. I went to Kansas City public school my entire life until my freshman year of high school. At the end of my eighth-grade year, the Kansas City School District lost its accreditation, which forced me and my family to make a decision on whether or not I was gonna stay in the Kansas City public school system and risk my high school diploma being meaningless to colleges or go to a private school which cost a good grip of money. But one of my older cousins on my father's side had been to that same school. It's called Rockhurst High School, an all-male institution. My cousin was a football star there and went on to play at University of Oklahoma during the early 2000s when they won all those national championships. To this day, he and I are probably the ones that our family look toward for continuing the legacy of building middle-class success in my family.

I went to Rockhurst, which was where all the rich white folks in Kansas City sent their sons. It was, and still is, one of the best schools in the nation for sports and academics. But for me, personally, it was where I recognized that white Kansas City and Black Kansas City were two totally fucking different things. The experiences that my white high school classmates lived every day were so far out of my reach, even with the success of my uncles, it was incomparable. We had totally different lifestyles, totally different access to resources. My friends in high school all had cars when they turned sixteen. And not just cars, but BMWs and Mercedes and Suburbans. They all traveled for holidays. They had lake houses and vacation homes and had been out of the country multiple times and their day-to-day life was just a different experience from mine.

I made one friend in particular at Rockhurst—Gil—who remains one of my best friends today. His family basically adopted me when it came to Rockhurst culture because his parents grew up humble in middle Missouri, where drugs are rampant. Some members of their family are still crackheads to this day. So they grew up modestly and worked hard to become very, very, very successful and very wealthy. In hindsight, I think they must have seen some of that work ethic in me and wanted their son to be around me, because they took me in. They are responsible for taking me out of the country for the first time in my life. They even paid for it, though my father was very hesitant to accept help or money from a white man. Gil's family took me on some of my first and best experiences of my life and just changed what I thought was the norm. They set a different precedent for what I wanted my norm to be for my family now and my future family.

Recognizing the difference between my life and theirs, and then taking real effort to insert myself into those new experiences is a pattern that I have pursued my entire professional career. I've had to be unafraid to take the chance to engulf myself into a new experience and to think holistically about what I can get out of it and how I'm gonna get it.

Chad: You touched on accessibility. In my experience, inroads to opportunities that gave me new ways to see the world—like

Google—have generally come from relationships with Black people. You mentioned Gil's family, from high school, who exposed you to new experiences. But have you been able to identify allies and Black champions for yourself in your career? Is that something you have worked on? Is that something you've gotten better at over time?

Jason: That has definitely been my experience. There have been allies throughout my professional career who didn't look like me, but I wish there were more. At Google, my mentors were Black people who put their arms around me in a way that made it comfortable because they recognized how difficult it was to be successful.

But in my first week at Google I was sitting in New York in the office with my manager, Kevin, who was white. I learned that I should always ask questions to make my managers feel good, so they would provide me with solutions. So I asked a question: "Hey, I'm really having a hard time learning people's names and you do such a good job of it. I always see you socializing with people. What's your secret?" And he started laughing. Then I realized that I was the only Black man in the entire building. And that's what I said, and he confirmed.

He said, "Yeah, that's why it's so easy for them to know your name because you are literally the only one here who looks like you."

At that point I stopped going to work looking for comfort or to feel comfortable. I went to work looking to work. That was my only thought. *I'm going to work and I'm going to work my ass off and I'm gonna work better than anybody else.* That was all I was thinking about. And I did. I worked hella hours. I was always the first one in and last one out. I wore a suit every day in the Google office, which nobody does. I needed to work and I needed to prove myself. I worked and that was all I did.

In terms of allies in the professional place, I think they're extremely important but I don't think I've figured it all out. I've been able to start and nurture relationships because I connect with people at their most vulnerable states of fun. Some people might call those vices instead of fun, but I like to look at those activities in a positive light. Those moments of smiles and laughter and energy are where I connect with people the best, whether they're older or younger. And those moments might take place at a bar or smoking a blunt and connecting or talking about nonprofessional things or whatever.

Being able to connect with people at that level helps them recognize my loyalty. They return that loyalty because I meet them at a vulnerable place—a positive, vulnerable place. A lot of my real relationships professionally started over fun. I had a meeting with one of my first managers from Google, who is now trying to recruit me to his team at Facebook. I remember getting drunk with him and writing on his face with a permanent marker as his intern. At the time we just laughed at it, but it was one of those nights where you build a bond forever.

I try to replicate that as much as possible.

Chad: But now you're far from an intern. Compared to when you started at Google as a twenty-year-old intern, how much of your cultural identity, how much of your full self, including your Blackness, do you bring into the work space? And how much do you lean into your Blackness now compared to ten years ago?

Jason: It's night-and-day different. Ten years ago, I did not bring my total Blackness into the workplace. I felt like my Black skin was probably too much for them to handle in the first place. They had to get comfortable with seeing my Black skin and not associating that with negativity or poor work or whatever bad thoughts prejudice puts in people's minds. I didn't feel comfortable enough being Black, which is one of the main reasons I think a lot of Blacks are not successful in tech companies—especially Googles and Amazons—because they don't feel accepted into the culture. The culture is not made for them. It's made for the masses of the white majority.

I didn't feel comfortable going into work and talking about my favorite type of hip-hop or talking about Black cultural events like Carnival or HBCU homecomings. I couldn't talk about that stuff because I didn't have anybody to talk to about that stuff. So much of my Blackness I either hid or I focused it where it was welcome. At Google, the Black Googler Network (BGN) was where I could focus my Blackness. It was like I was Black Jason outside of Google and inside I was whoever they wanted me to be. But with my BGN friends I was Black through and through, because in BGN I found cultural acceptance. I recognized in those environments I stood out, not because I was more Black than anybody else, but because I was Black and I was observant of our white surroundings and I was able to kind of bridge those two things together.

The difference between who I am now and who I was then is that through my career, I have continued to see the value in my Blackness and the value of that perspective. I've also learned that, in being entrepreneurial and starting Partpic, I *shouldn't* hide my Blackness. I *should* talk about Black things. I recognize that I am a Black founder with a diverse team of Black and white employees, and when I was at Google my white colleagues didn't try to hide their culture from me. At Rockhurst, they didn't try to be Black for me or show me Blackness, they only showed me what they knew—which was their white privilege. Which is fine, I don't judge them for that. That's not their fault that they were born into that position, but the point is they don't tiptoe around their whiteness. And as a founder, now I don't have to either.

The Wiz is my favorite movie. I made a point to encourage my employees to watch it. While it might be a minor example, it's an example of something I wouldn't feel comfortable as an employee at Google saying early in my career. But now I have no problem asking what Black Lives Matters means to my employees or leading those kinds of conversations. When we started Partpic, we did those things. We played hip-hop music in the office. It was just this idea of recognizing that we are Black. We're not going to hide the fact that we're Black, and while that may be uncomfortable to some people, evidence of Blackness is not a bad thing. And I'm going to keep pushing you. And you might be uncomfortable, but it's coming from a place of giving people access and a viewpoint into the world of Blackness and the people that are shunned because of their Blackness. So, today I am much more confident in the idea of who I am and what value I bring because of my Blackness.

Chad: Think about a Black twenty-one-year-old coming into adulthood realizing she's in charge of shaping her future. Where can that person find comfort, advantage, leverage, strength? Where can she find that within her Blackness? Where would you say, "This is where your identity can create advantages for you"?

Jason: That's a difficult question because of how diverse we are as Black people and because of all the things we need as individuals. We all need different things to be successful. Some people just lack confidence. Other people lack skills. Others lack other things. But to identify that one source of strength or truth for Black kids, I would first say family. For me it was family and faith. So that's how I did it. It was the fact that my family, even my mom's side of the family that was all fucked up, what they did believe in was being a family and holding each other down. Regardless of what they did and who they did it with, at the end of the day we had a family bond.

My father's side was responsible for giving me faith and religion and spirituality. That's where I found confidence, but every Black kid doesn't have that.

I live by the phrase *know thyself and live accordingly*. That phrase has meant something different to me as I've grown up. Especially the *live accordingly* piece. So, I would say: anchor yourself in you. Anchor in asking yourself who you are, what you want, and what you're willing to do to get it. If people ask themselves those questions and are truthful about the answers, I think the identity of self can become strong enough to appeal to outsiders in a way that creates opportunity. If you're doing something you love and if you are passionate about what you're doing, people will see. Once people see, then you become accessible to other perspectives, ideas, and experiences.

That access to new perspectives creates more opportunities. But first it starts with you. Nobody can be you for you. You have to do that on your own.

DR. LYNN MCKINLEY-GRANT

"There's a double-edged sword. They used to make you feel inferior just because you were Black. But now they try to make you feel inferior because you may be more educated than them. They've been duped by the Trumps of the world and the white privileged men."

Dr. McKinley-Grant earned her MD at Harvard Medical School. She is a board-certified dermatologist, author, researcher, and associate professor of Dermatology at Howard University College of Medicine. Dr. McKinley-Grant has practiced dermatology for over twenty-five years in Washington, DC. She is president of the Skin of Color Society and a member of the American Academy of Dermatology and National Medical Association and has been listed in *Washingtonian* magazine as one of the area's "Top Doctors." Her special area of interest is using the arts to train physicians in making accurate diagnoses in all skin colors.

But for most of my life I've known Dr. Grant as Aunt Lynn. Her daughter and my older sister went to preschool together, and our families have maintained a friendship across the DC/Maryland border for three decades. The Grants were always a force in the DC metro area; a regal Black family living in a beautiful brick house striped with growing ivy.

Every Christmas Eve my parents, my sister, and I would load into my dad's Acura SUV and take the thirty-minute drive into the city to park among the BMWs, Lexuses, and Mercedes-Benzes lined out front the Grants' house.

Inside, Dr. Lynn and Dr. David Grant and their daughter Davlyn would greet us with warm apple cider and sweet potato pie. The house was full of Black professionals and their families loudly singing "The Twelve Days of Christmas."

Sometimes I felt a little out of place at the parties, because I thought the 16th Street Black people who lived in DC were richer and more proper than us suburbanites. But then Dr. Grant's friends, who'd migrated from Harlem down to DC, would come in, dressed to the nines, and *truly* party. I didn't feel out of place then; I felt happy and entertained. After a few spiked ciders, some would break into their version of "Theme from *New York, New York*," complete with eye-high Rockette kicks.

Black doctors, lawyers, dentists, professors, politicians, musicians, engineers . . . they all came through to celebrate. The wine flowed from eight until the last few families trickled out after midnight, and I wondered, What were they celebrating? Why were they so happy to see each other? Why so many cheek kisses and hugs and joyful shrieks to accompany the off-key Christmas carols?

Based on my observation of Dr. Grant and her friends, I thought Harlem must be some place where all the Black people were rich and well dressed and well educated. In our interview Dr. Grant set me straight. She informed me that Black people in Harlem in the fifties struggled just like Black people everywhere else. But the advantage her neighborhood offered was its community and the high expectations that community instilled in its young people. There was an explicit agreement among

Harlemites at that time that children would excel academically and professionally, and that would lead them to give back to the community. Dr. Grant was taught by example by her mother and her neighbors. That's why Dr. Grant hosted Christmas Eve every year, to make sure we as Black kids with opportunity, surrounded by white people at school, knew our elders, and knew that they would hold us to the same high expectations.

In Harlem, Dr. Grant learned that Black Magic is passed on within communities. In DC, on Christmas Eve, she made sure to share that magic with the next generation.

Chad: So what do you do and how were you educated, Dr. Grant?

Lynn: I am a dermatologist and an internist. For most of my career I have taken care of patients but combined that in an academic setting with teaching. And some writing also. I went to college and medical school, did the whole thing. Growing up I was in New York and then we moved to Washington and then we moved back to New York. So there were always changes in schools. I went from first year in public school, and a teacher yelled at me or something so my mother put me in Catholic school. In Catholic school the teachers would beat you, but it was a very good structured education, you know.

In fourth grade I was taken out of Catholic school because I wanted to become Catholic and we were Episcopal, so that wasn't going to work. So I ended up going to a private school where you called the teachers by their first names. It was a very liberal school in New York. I was just in elementary school then.

And then we moved to Washington, DC. Something that triggered me was that I realized in New York I really grew up in an all-Black community. I grew up in Harlem, you know. My family is Black, educated. White people existed, but they really weren't a big part of my life until I went to private school. And then I really thought all white people were Jewish, because that's New York, you know. So I learned more about the Jewish culture.

But most communities weren't integrated. A lot of my strength and the expectations I had for myself came from the housing complex I lived in. It was a group of very highly educated Black people who were leaders in the community. There was a guy who was an executive at Macy's and this was in the fifties. In that community excellence was just expected of you. There was no question about whether you were going to college, because your parents went to college. You knew you were going someplace.

I had someone ask me once, "Why do you keep doing more stuff? You've done so much. Why don't you just stop?" I don't know why I never stopped. That's something for a psychiatrist to deal with.

Anyway, we moved to Washington when I was in seventh grade and then we moved back to New York and I had to finish school in New York. In New York, to get an academic diploma, you have to do Regents exams. I had to do them all in one year. Most people do it in four years—languages, science, math, history. I got them all done in a year.

At that point I was at an integrated high school in New York, and when it came time to fill out college applications the school told me I wasn't college material and that I really needed to go to trade school to be a secretary. They said I should be a stenographer or something. They wouldn't send my applications to colleges. All my friends were applying to Harvard and Yale and blah, blah, blah. So, I sent in my own applications. I didn't do Harvard and Yale, but I did some of the other schools, like Boston University and Syracuse. But the people running my own school said they didn't feel that I should go to college. That *infuriated* my parents. So I ended up going to Fisk University, which was another great opportunity. But I decided to go on exchange to Colby College because all my friends from high school were going to white schools so I said—well, let me go to Colby.

That was an academic shock coming from Fisk, but I really learned how to study. I majored in Political Science. It was the sixties and I was a revolutionary person. I wanted to "change the world." When I got back to New York I was part of the Civil Rights Movement but stayed in education—counseling kids about going to college and stuff. I ended up getting a master's in Counseling. I was counseling college students who were going into medicine and law and I thought that was interesting. So, I ended up going to medical school. I had a friend who was very ill and I just thought, "Well maybe medicine. Maybe I should give medicine a try."

Chad: Got it. You mentioned a couple things I want to explore. You said that the expectation in your mostly Black community in Harlem was that you would do great things. How were those expectations communicated? How were they instilled? How did they stay with you when you moved out of all-Black communities?

Lynn: There were times I know my mother was struggling financially, but I never considered us poor because she was still working and she worked at the YMCA in public relations. We were both very involved in the Civil Rights Movement, so there was always this thing about giving back and I did volunteer work at Harlem Hospital. We were always helping somebody with something. Because there were always people who were less fortunate than us.

I always felt that our family was kind of important in the community. People would see me and say "well this is Aretha's daughter." That meant something important. So I had to really act like I had some sense. The people that we were around, even socially, they really worked hard and so you were expected to study hard. Books were always around. I remember Marian Wright Edelman saying that she could get out of doing chores if she was reading a book. And sometimes that would work in my house.

There were always these opportunities to learn and exposure to new things. We got to take advantage of experiences outside of Harlem. We would go to museums. We would go to concerts. We would do stuff at home. On Sundays, families would get together and somebody always had a piano, so there was singing, and it would be after church so you couldn't go shopping or anything. Or you'd read poetry. I can remember times of us sitting around reading poetry to each other. First the kids would read some aloud and then the adults would read some. One of Countee Cullen's wives was one of my mother's good friends and so we had that kind of exposure. And just listening. A lot of times as a child you didn't say anything. You just kind of sat and listened to what people were talking about and the struggles they had, but they didn't talk about that as much.

Chad: I'm writing this book because of my experience starting my career at Google after moving from Atlanta to Silicon Valley. I was working in a nearly entirely white and Asian office and dealing with my learning curves in the ways people engaged with each other and how they talked about work. I was trying to understand the social habits outside the office, and all of this was a gigantic culture shock for me.

I'm writing this book to learn, from people like you, how to find power in our Blackness instead of weakness or isolation.

If a young aspiring doctor grabs this book and flips to your section, what do you want her to find?

Lynn: I would want her to know that she is somebody. That's really important, because you can lose that. And it's really different now. White privilege can make white people think you're taking away something from them. I realize that is the biggest source of prejudice that's happening in terms of racism. It's the fact that they feel that you've done well and because you've done well they are not doing well. So they're blaming that on you and you happen to be Black too. There's a double-edged sword. They used to make you feel inferior just because you were Black. But now they try to make you feel inferior because you may be more educated than them. They've been duped by the Trumps of the world and the white privileged men.

So, my message to a young person opening this book is that they are somebody. Maya Angelou used to talk about the importance of the sense of belonging. The way I've interpreted

Maya Angelou's message is that you can't be free if you feel like you have to belong someplace. She says, "You only are free when you realize you belong no place—you belong every place—no place at all. The price is high. The reward is great."* She talks about really being free and that means kind of being who you are and it sometimes means that you don't belong; not that you shouldn't be there, you need to be there, but you won't feel a part of belonging. It takes maturity to be comfortable with that.

Growing up in New York, and in Jack and Jill, I was the darkest person in the group. Because of that, I didn't have a sense of belonging. And then when I was at Duke—I was Black, I was a woman. I didn't belong. Having a sense that you are somebody, that you're important, that you belong wherever you are matters. We each have an experience to bring.

TARLIN RAY

"If I think about my professional career, there has been no mentor in any environment that looks like me."

Tarlin is an education and technology executive, investor, startup advisor, and former Division 1 college basketball player. Today he is the senior vice president of business development and product management at Kaplan North America. Formerly, he was president of Dev Bootcamp—the world's first immersive

---

* "You only are free when you realize you belong no place—you belong every place—no place at all" (Maya Angelou, *Conversations with Maya Angelou*, ed. Jeffrey M. Elliott [Jackson, MS: University Press of Mississippi, 1989]).

coding bootcamp. Tarlin earned his MBA at Harvard Business School and his AB in Economics at Harvard University, where he played on the basketball team. He grew up in the town of Brentwood in Los Angeles.

I first met Tarlin when I was working for a small tech startup that was bought by Kaplan. Tarlin was sent over from the mothership to take command of our startup, a small coding school that was leaking money. His job, from what I could tell, was to figure out how to make our business profitable or close us down. Tarlin was clean-shaven, sharp. He usually wore starched collared shirts. As an executive, he had clout with Kaplan and they trusted him to take on major projects like our startup. Most of the overlords at Kaplan seemed to be old, bald white guys, and they seemed very comfortable with Tarlin. So I read Tarlin as a company man. That's actually why I thought Tarlin would be a great mentor. I too wanted to be well paid and trusted by my superiors at the company. I asked Tarlin to grab coffee because I wanted to learn how to climb the corporate ranks. He was generous with his time and knowledge.

When we sat down, Tarlin asked *me* a question I had on my list of questions for *him*: "So what are you doing here, Black man?" I gave him the Silicon Valley, jargon-y answer. I said I was trying to change the world and make some money. I never got around to flipping the question back on him, so I did, many coffee chats later, when I asked him to participate in this book.

What was he, a Black man from LA, doing in the places he'd been? First Brentwood, an affluent LA suburb. Then Harvard Business School and now the executive ranks of Kaplan,

Inc. Tarlin described his upbringing in a two-parent household, with money. I liked how Tarlin owned his privilege. He called out his good fortune. He didn't pretend to come from a disadvantaged background. But still Tarlin accepted his mission to help other Black people who started with less, and stressed that he will teach his daughters to do the same.

And yet, as he moved from place to place, Tarlin had no Black mentors on his way up. It seems impossible to me. How did he have the confidence to push through glass ceilings without learning from others who had done it before him? I discovered he learned his values from his parents at home growing up in Brentwood. Tarlin's Black Magic is self-awareness and sending the elevator back down. He understands the rarity of the advantages he was born into compared to so many other Black people, and he uses his positioning near the top of the corporate ladder to help others—like me—find their way through the maze.

———

Tarlin: I grew up in Ladera Heights and then when I was in seventh grade my folks moved us to Brentwood.

Chad: What was it like growing up as a Black kid in Brentwood? How did you end up as a student athlete at Harvard?

Tarlin: I just need to start with my folks. Both of my parents are from Ohio. My father was one of seven children. You know, the bathroom was an outhouse and he slept in the same bed with his two older brothers. Both of my parents were the first generation to go to college. I was lucky to have them as role models who paved the way for me to understand how to navigate a world where I'm often one of few individuals that look like me.

My mom was one of the first teachers in her magnet school in Los Angeles. Education was important. My dad was the first Black partner in a major law firm in LA. My dad went to Howard University for law school. One day he made a decision, based on weather, to move the family from Washington, DC, to LA. He was sick of fighting winters and there was an opportunity to go to a major firm.

You asked what it was like to grow up in Brentwood. I would not have been able to handle what was a very homogenous, very affluent environment, without watching my parents navigate being the "only ones"; without watching them navigate how to work with power and gather their own power and create a team-tribe around them. That tribe was made up of other Black folks in Los Angeles who were doctors or lawyers working in entertainment who launched their own businesses. I got to watch and learn from them as well.

So when I got to grade school and I was one of only six Black males in class, I didn't feel like I was ostracized. We had our tribe. We had our Black student union.

But it didn't feel like anything could hold me back from taking full advantage of the opportunities there, whether it was student government or playing two sports or being an admissions counselor or writing for the paper. My parents enabled me to feel comfortable, and even though it was a very homogenous environment, as I applied to colleges I felt that anything was possible. I had worked hard, and had a work ethic coming from my folks. I tried a bunch of things in school that were passions for me. I created what I felt was a legitimate

CV to go to some of the best schools. I felt like I could hang with anyone.

Chad: You mentioned how your parents grew up. You said your dad grew up sharing a bed with two of his brothers. My father had a very similar experience growing up in Detroit. I just had another conversation with a really close friend from college whose uncle on his mom's side was shot and killed at a family get-together. Across these conversations for the book, everyone mentions being one degree away from tragedy or poverty. How close or far away does that feel to you? How much time do you spend remembering where your family comes from?

Tarlin: I don't feel like that place is close. What I do know is that I'm extraordinarily fortunate.

There's just luck that is involved. I think about my mom's side—you know, super-talented side of the family—but they've had some struggles. My dad's side, his hometown in Ohio used to be a thriving community because there was industry there. Then the factories left. Now it's known for its two or three prisons, one of which was the prison highlighted in *The Shawshank Redemption*. So I know that I am extraordinarily fortunate to have the opportunity I have, which is why I probably still push hard to not waste that opportunity. Granted, everyone has to work hard. You're not handed anything.

So I spend less time thinking about how close I am to tragedy or poverty because I'm probably further away. While I was a child and growing up I was probably shielded more from that one degree, unless we were going on a plane to Ohio and hearing some of the stories that our relatives were going through. But I think I'm channeling an extremely rare and lucky opportunity.

When I'm talking to my daughters—I have an eleven- and an eight-year-old—I make sure they know nothing should be handed to them and they should go and give back to communities that are not as fortunate. Because we want to make sure we not only give my girls opportunity, but make sure they are service-oriented in the future. Because we need to spread "the luck" to more people, so they feel as emboldened and empowered as I felt growing up.

Chad: When we worked together, my boss, who was a white guy, said, "You're going to be working with this guy Tarlin and you're gonna love him." He kinda had this look on his face. So I thought, *Okay, I know what this means. Tarlin is Black.* I met you, and indeed you were Black and I loved you. I felt immediately a different level of trust than the trust I had with other colleagues. I could tell you what I felt. I could tell you where I was coming from in a way that was different for me than my relationships with most of my colleagues. I've had similar experiences with other Black colleagues. Most of the times I've found that a door I wasn't yet qualified to walk through was opened up by someone Black who is older than me.

Have you had a similar experience? Have you found Black people to open doors that you didn't expect to open?

Tarlin: If I think about my professional career, there has been no mentor in any environment that looks like me. I've spent a lot of time in early stage companies. If you look at venture capital, especially in the early 2000s, there were not a lot of Black executives or Black senior leaders. There wasn't a nod. There was no "let's go to coffee." Oftentimes the doors opened from individuals who did not look like me. Which meant that

I had to fall back on my ability to relate to people who didn't look like me, which came from the grooming I had growing up the way I did.

I am currently the most senior Black executive at a large, public education company and there is no one I've interacted with broadly that looks like me. I've always had a peer set but to have a mentor to help me grow, I've often had to look out and not within the company.

Chad: So for anyone else who is Black looking up to you at that company, you look like the glass ceiling to them. Does it feel that way to you?

Tarlin: So I'm the glass ceiling only if I place limits on what I want to do.

Chad: I could see someone looking up and saying, "Tarlin has reached this level in the company. It appears that is the highest level that someone like me can reach within this company. That looks like the glass ceiling to me." Does it feel that way to you? Has that seeped into your own mindset?

Tarlin: No. Maybe this is just the nature of the work I'm doing.

I left Kaplan after climbing the ladder to go pursue an entrepreneurial venture that I felt was more growth-oriented. I came back to Kaplan to go to a startup born out of Kaplan to build something. So for me, the ceiling is only on what I believe are the opportunities out there, and my ability to partner with an organization to see if I can get supported and funded to do those things. It's less about someone in a seat.

I feel unencumbered because I feel supported by the CEO and COO to go do this thing. But other individuals in the organization don't know that. So the last thing they saw was Tarlin, a very senior guy, running a division of Kaplan and closing it down. They have no idea what's happened since.

I think about work in a different way. There are people who are prone to want to be the leader of a large organization. Those are a small subset. I'm more passionate about trying to build something out of the thought leadership and concepts I think are worthwhile, and then organize a movement around that rather than taking over what already exists.

Chad: Why do you think you're built to build instead of assuming an already existing position?

Tarlin: For a while I wanted to study second-generation Black children of white-collar families. [My parents] went through the trials and tribulations of proving they could perform. They had to make partner, all that. And once that happens, you get exposed to yes, being a doctor or lawyer is a path you can take. But there is so much more you can do to be self-actualized, to make money, to make a difference. So there was no limit put on me. My wife's parents immigrated from China, so there was a fixed mindset about the type of work you do to be successful. Other than making sure I got the best education, there were never any other fixed boundaries to stop me from dreaming.

When I was eleven, for two years we moved to New York. My dad was setting up a branch of a law firm in New York. In my fourth-grade class we ran a pizza business. I was the treasurer raising the money for our business. We sent out our salespeople to sell tickets. We'd get the money back, we'd buy pizza wholesale and then distribute the pizza at school on Fridays. Whatever surplus we had we used to go on a trip at the end of the year. I got excited about business and I learned the word "entrepreneur." You can be your own boss. It's about how you can take an idea and have fun with it. My parents pushed me to get the right foundation, and I felt like with that grooming there were so many more possibilities for me than what I saw.

I had another friend—who was the son of a partner at my dad's firm—who was on *Survivor*. Does the world become more of your oyster because of the initial foundation you get, because your parents have broken the glass ceiling—and therefore there's more to life?

Chad: Is there anything valuable that you learned from your experience as a Black man growing up the way you did that helps you in your work?

Tarlin: I believe being able to communicate is a unique kung fu that gives you a continued way to advance. I'm talking about written and verbal communication. I believe with technology tools we are losing that ability to communicate, thus losing the opportunity to learn how to persuade and to engage and to debate. My dad considered asking me a ton of questions to be small talk, but it felt like the third degree. My dad would ask five questions about anything I said I learned or believed, to make sure my argument was sound and tight. I think that ability to articulate ideas—even if you don't look like everyone in the room—will at least get everyone to pay attention. I think that's something that's being lost.

People do a quick assessment of you. I try to show up so that someone cannot make a determination of who I am *before* they get to hear what I have to say. I don't ever want to mute someone's artistry or their style, but, depending on the environment,

I think it's helpful to remove bias. Remove bias and then get a chance to show them what you really think. To me, that means continue to hone your craft and your communication style, verbally—whether forcing yourself to do presentations, or sitting around the dining room table talking about your day with your children. As they're communicating, pick their message apart and tell them better ways they could package messages. I believe that is massively important, especially for young Black men and women, because it opens a ton of doors.

Don't limit yourself to 140 characters. Force yourself to write things long form. Force yourself to write even longer letters. That will help with whatever you do for the rest of your life.

Chapter Two

GRADE SCHOOL: GIFTED AND TALENTED PROGRAMS, PRIVATE SCHOOL, AND SEPARATION

"The only thing that interferes with my learning is my education."

—Albert Einstein

In first grade, not long after my family moved to that cul-de-sac, I tested into Montgomery County's Gifted and Talented academic track, which meant that I would be surrounded by white people in classrooms for the rest of grade school. Later I realized how common this experience is for Black students who test well. In conversations with my classmates at Morehouse years later, we'd discuss how at young ages we were plucked from Black classrooms, Black sports teams, and Black neighborhoods and placed into white environments like "Gifted and Talented" magnet schools, expensive prep schools, club sports teams, and selective music programs.

My parents and the parents of my Black classmates were

willing to submit their kids to these white environments so that we could have access to resources, from modern curriculums to broader networks.

But there is a trade-off. The most discerning parents recognize this trade-off. My parents did. They knew that I would suffer from the jarring transition. There was a chance I would be the only Black child in my Gifted and Talented program. I would be alone. For Jewel Burks, who I interview later in this book, this transition meant being removed from environments full of people who looked like her and being pushed into places where there were more resources, but where her hair and her way of speaking and her very self were harshly scrutinized. I would also be subjected to the burn of subtle racism and the blaze of overt racism to gain access to more promising academic, career, and financial opportunities. That would introduce risks to my safety, both emotionally and physically, in ways I couldn't then imagine or articulate.

Some parents try to offset the trauma of this experience with at-home education. My parents, in addition to their rules, made a point to review what I was taught academically and socially, to offer context and corrections. They taught me about Black history undistorted by whitewashed curriculums. They asked me questions about how the other kids and the teachers treated me. They refilled my little tank of self-esteem with love. Every morning before school and every night at dinner my parents dug into these lessons.

"Did your teacher mention the free Black explorers who traveled to the Americas from Africa, or only slaves?"

"You know the Egyptians were great mathematicians. Did Mr. Ryan mention that in Geometry?"

I remember my mom once asked my sister, "Why do you think Kate cares so much whether or not you wear a shower cap in the pool? Maybe she wishes her hair was curly like yours."

There are other kinds of Black parents. Many Black parents believe their children's white teachers and classmates see them for who they are, separate from their Blackness, and will love them. They believe that their kids will live safe and happy lives because of that white acceptance. I remember listening to Jack and Jill parents brag at fancy get-togethers about their children being accepted at DC prep schools like National Cathedral School or Saint Albans or Sidwell Friends, where they'd leave behind their peers at the DC public schools to get a real chance to excel. Their children eventually mimicked the parents' enthusiasm for white acceptance. Today, as we enter our mid-thirties, many of them still struggle with their racial identity. Others continue to try to escape their race. Grayson Brown, who I spoke to for this book, admits he finally stopped chasing white acceptance when he was expelled from a mostly white liberal arts college, as a result of a traumatic and racially charged conflict—where he was wronged. Many never have such a reckoning, and still complain of the emptiness they feel surrounded by whiteness in corporate jobs and gentrifying communities, disconnected from people who look like them. They were uprooted in the name of upward mobility and now find themselves trapped again.

❖ ❖

I was five years old when I first realized how race made me different from, and in some ways a target for, the white kids around me in my Montessori preschool. My best friend was a blond-haired kid named Eric. My parents allowed me to sleep over at his house because his parents were kind-spirited Silver Spring hippies who welcomed my folks to make regular check-ins over the course of the night. When it was time to go to sleep, we'd build pillow forts on the living room couches and pretend that we were camping outside.

One night, after we built a pillow fort, we caught a network TV airing of Spike Lee's *Malcolm X*. We knew our parents wouldn't have let us watch, but we didn't change the channel. I saw hate crimes against Black people for the first time in visual form. The scene in which Malcolm X's father is tied to train tracks was forever etched in my brain. The actor's terrified howling still rings in my ears at times. I was scared, and riveted. The man's crime was Blackness and the punishment was death by train, levied by hooded white terrorists. The message was clear: as a Black person I should always feel afraid of whiteness and be certain to kowtow to white people. I understood even as a small child.

Eric's parents must have heard the television because his mom came downstairs in her robe and turned off the movie and unplugged the cord. Too late. I was changed. In minutes Eric was asleep on his tiny section of the pillow fort. I pulled my first all-nighter, tossing and turning in my Snoopy T-shirt, worrying that I'd been tricked. I feared Eric's family was going to hand me over to the hooded terrorists I'd seen in the movie. They didn't, but the intrinsic trust I once had in them—in all people, just because they were people—was broken. It's been a lifelong exercise trying to restore that intrinsic trust. I felt alone and unsafe.

That feeling resurfaced later that year. One day, at naptime, my teacher Ms. Leinhardt put a movie on with the volume down at a low hum to soothe us.

As was our ritual, Eric and I pulled our sleeping mats close together. The classroom was filled with boxes of colorful Legos. Forest animal posters on the walls. Bright, shiny streamers dangled from the ceilings, hung with nontoxic glue in case we ate them. We had a class pet rabbit. We were empowered to structure our own days as we wanted. We never had to ask to go to the bathroom and recess was optional. I felt safe in that classroom until this particular day.

Eric and I whispered about our plans for the Lego spaceship we were building to replicate Han Solo's Millennium Falcon. We would usually talk until one of us fell asleep, and then the other would drift off. But today Eric had something on his mind. I could tell by the smirk on his face he was going to say something he knew he shouldn't. I now recognize this face on white people as a glaring caution sign; it precedes a breach of trust.

"Black people kind of look like poop."

The words almost make me laugh now. But at the time my little heart sank. What he said was absurd. But as a kid I could recognize by his tone that he was trying to hurt me.

My parents had already begun to teach me about race. I knew I wasn't supposed to laugh at his words. But I did. Even though he was trying to hurt me, I wanted to make *him* comfortable. I wanted to stay connected to my friend. I was scared of losing him.

I spat back the quickest comeback I could find. I said his hair was dirty, but there was no force in my voice. He didn't even hear me. He was too busy laughing at his own joke, emboldened by my own laughter. I sacrificed myself to affirm him.

Eric rolled over on his mat and was asleep in seconds. I lay there stewing. I looked around and noticed for the first time that there were no other Black kids in the class. I saw all the peacefully sleeping white faces, my teacher quietly reading at her desk, the droning white man on the boxy nineties RCA television, and then Eric right next to me. I would be the only Black kid in nearly all my classes for the rest of elementary school, middle school, and high school.

That night at the dinner table, my mom recounted her day at Verizon, still in her pantsuit, stylish necklace, watch, and bracelets. We were eating fried fish and greens, my dad's specialty. My sister was hiding a book under the dinner table, pushing up her plastic red glasses. "Living for the City" by Stevie Wonder was playing from the stereo of a CD player. When my mom reached a break in her story I just blurted out the words:

"Black people kind of look like poop," I said.

My dad and sister shifted in their seats, both turning their focus to me. But it was my mom who spoke first.

"What, Chad?" she said. The corners of her mouth turned up but not in a smile. More like the annoyed look you give when you turn onto the freeway and realize the fries you ordered at the drive-through aren't in the bag. Her eyes narrowed.

"Eric said that to me at school today," I said. I stared down at the table. I didn't really know *why* I had told them; I knew I was supposed to.

"Eric Boil said that?" she said. "You hear this, Bruce? Chad, when white people say things like that they're trying to shake you up. You should have told Eric . . ."

My sister closed her book. She found this moment more interesting than the story in its pages. My mom continued. She instructed that when these things happened I should embrace confrontation. It was my responsibility to not let Eric get away with being an asshole. If I let him slide once, he was going to continue to kick me over and over again until nothing remained of my self-esteem.

By the time my mom took a breath from her ten-minute spiel on how to deal with paper-cut racism, my father had walked out and returned to the kitchen table with a copy of *The Souls of Black Folk* by W. E. B. DuBois. My sister and I would do a read-aloud. I came to think of these sorts of books as a Black parent's first aid kit.

"Remember Chad," my dad said, "Africa was the origin of human philosophy and you're named after the country Chad in the center of Africa."

I wasn't sure how we arrived at this place from a comment about poop. But this sort of cultural affirming was common in my house anytime one of us—my sister and I at school, my mom or dad at work—reported anything close to racism. It didn't protect us entirely, but it healed us. It took me years to find the stomach to address people like Eric head-on.

◆ ◆

That moment with Eric at naptime in preschool was the first time I felt isolated in school, but it wasn't the last. I was isolated both from my peers and my teachers. From preschool to high school, my only consistent classmate of color was a Puerto Rican–American girl named Alicia who became a close friend as we weathered the storm of representing all people of color in our classes together. I never had a Black male teacher in a non–physical education class. I was rarely taught by Black women. At the time, I assumed that all teachers were white.

My high school basketball coach, Damon Pigrom, was Black. He'd played college ball at Hampton University. He was gruff and honest and cared deeply about me and my teammates. He demanded more from us than anyone I've worked for since. On the day of my Morehouse College interview as a senior in high school, Coach Pigrom saw me heading to meet with Morehouse's dean of students, who had come to Silver Spring to decide which Black boys to offer scholarship money. I was wearing a wrinkled, untucked polo shirt. Coach commanded me to go home and put on a tie and a decent shirt before my meeting. I followed his orders and I was awarded a full scholarship after my interview. I think Coach's advice saved me thousands of dollars in college loans. I'm left to wonder how my experience would have differed had I been taught by two or three Coach Pigroms in classrooms; people who connected with me and felt invested in me. I often consider what must have been missing between me and my teachers because of our identity differences, and how that must have disadvantaged me compared to my classmates.

Instead I seethed my way through classes, like History where my sixth-grade teacher called slavery an "economically savvy historical inconvenience." He didn't invent that. Our History textbooks, published in the nineties, used inhumane terms. One listed the positives and negatives of slavery's impacts visually in equal proportion on opposite sides of a vertical line running down the length of the page. Even English, my favorite class, was a battle because of race. I slumped and contorted and snarled and cowered as my classmates plowed through the word "nigger" when we read *Huckleberry Finn* aloud in seventh grade.

The curriculum frustrated and marginalized me, but I pushed myself to do the work. The work didn't just mean homework—I was more interested in winning arguments against my class-mates than learning. They took turns arguing me down on why the word "nigger" was important to the text and why it should be okay for them to speak it when quoting such an important story. I didn't want them to beat me.

I spent so much energy being the lone spokesman for Blackness in every class. It was energy I could have spent learn-ing. I was a good student, but I was never an excellent stu-dent—in part because I was always engaged in cultural battles on top of my course work. That's too much for one kid. But I thought that conceding would mean both that my classmates were right *and* that they were smarter than I was. And, after all, my mother had told me when I was only five not to let people like Eric slide. I couldn't look my parents in the eye at dinner knowing I'd been a coward in class. So when I felt I had the moral high ground—Lord—I was tenacious.

Between classes, I retreated to the hallways, where I could find my basketball teammates. They were Black. They loved me. They accepted me. I'd clumsily try to code-switch from the King's English I used in class to a colloquial "Black" tone with my friends. It was probably insulting, but they never called me on it. I didn't respect my friends enough to realize that they could understand the ways we were different. I thought there was one way to be Black and I needed to project it to hold on to my friendships. I projected on my friends and others the shame I felt for this. I carried tension from jostling with whiteness for seven fifty-minute periods each day and then walked out of class and levied my discomfort on the people closest to me. I was biting and condescending. Anytime I got into an argument with a friend, I would try to make him feel small in the same way I felt bullied in my classrooms. One tactic I learned in those classes was to interject with grammar corrections to slow down the momentum of a competing argument. I corrected one of my best friends in the locker room before a game when he misused the word "comprised" in an argument. He slammed me against a trash bin. Much deserved.

When the bell rang, signaling the beginning of the next period, my jaw tightened and I'd shuffle from the hallway to my next class for another round. Advanced Placement Math. Once, I accidentally let slip a few words swirling in my head from Jay-Z's *The Blueprint* album during a quiet testing period. A girl yelled out from three rows back.

"What are you, trying to sound *Black*?" she said. I still cringe.

My code-switching felt necessary because I saw the way Black students were silenced in class if they didn't speak with a tone and vocabulary to match the white kids and teachers. This was before "diversity" was en vogue and before companies were using Black culture to sell products so enthusiastically. What that meant in my classrooms was I needed to sound "articulate" for my point of view to be taken seriously. In Social Studies class I had a biracial classmate named Keith who scored higher on tests than I did, but he spoke in broken English and was thus talked over by our classmates. I saw in his slumping posture how it wore on him each time he was drowned out in group discussion. He gave up eventually and became a spectator.

◆ ◆

Racial isolation became just as pronounced outside of school as it was inside. In my junior year of high school my basketball team made it all the way to the Maryland 4A State Championship.

This event took over our school, transforming it into the real-life *Friday Night Lights*. Fans from all over the county packed out our standing room only games. Local media squeezed onto the baseline to take photos to run in the *Washington Post* and the *Gazette*. We felt like celebrities for a season.

I learned how ravenously whiteness engulfs those who offer value, like we did. I finally felt accepted as a peer by my classmates. They wanted me around. They wanted to hear what I had to say. They challenged my point of view less in class, and even inflated my ego. I relished their adoration. I quickly forgot how just months earlier they had silenced and belittled and isolated me. On a small scale, I understood how hugely successful Black performers like Kanye West get lost in echo chambers of white applause.

Suddenly, I was invited to parties at giant houses in Olney and Potomac, where my wealthy classmates lived. I was surprised, when I showed up, to learn that the white parents were often out of town on those nights. When they were present, they would allow or even encourage heavy drinking. They would look the other way when kids used more dangerous drugs. They offered mostly free rein for up to fifty drunken high schoolers in their expensive homes.

There was one concrete rule across several of the houses: no more than two Black kids in the house at a time. It was an unwritten rule but I faced it often. The rule was communicated by the kids of the hosting households and never by the parents. Those kids would twist up their faces to remind us when we'd reached maximum capacity on Black guests, then awkwardly turn back into the fray of the party. Sometimes exceptions to the "2 Black kids rule" were made for the basketball team. Every now and then the kids of the house would help us sneak a few of the guys around through the backyard to avoid watchful parents.

These were large four- or five-story houses, set on an acre or two of land; a forty-five-minute drive to the Capitol, a twenty-five-minute drive to farmlands, rolling hills, and scattered Confederate flags on the backs of pickup trucks. As we entered the gated communities, my teammates and I would turn down our blaring music—back then it was 50 Cent or Three 6 Mafia—and park along the street leading up to the house. We usually walked to the back door, but if we went in through the front, a middle-aged dad would meet us there, beer in hand. He'd look us up and down until he recognized the tallest of us from our last basketball game. Then a huge smile would spread over his face. He might offer us a beer himself or lead us into the kitchen, where we'd find our classmates laughing, chugging, smiling, welcoming us into their world. I find it ironic now that they too were blasting 50 Cent during parties where only two Black people were allowed at a time.

In the basement, we'd find more of our white classmates, steering harder into the night than the kids upstairs. Some downing shots, some sneaking into back rooms to hook up, others experimenting with cocaine and pills. I avoided them. My parents' judgment was a much stronger force than peer pressure at that time. I'd usually find my way out to the backyard, where a few kids were sitting around a bonfire. I remember the bonfires still. They stood out. Something about them felt like such a statement of white privilege. The space. The smoke. The consuming flame.

"You guys can make fires in your backyard? Just because?"

I never actually asked the question, but damn.

We knew there weren't supposed to be a bunch of Black kids here, a place that had a huge backyard and a bonfire, but sometimes we'd plead to exceed the maximum capacity on Black kids in the party so a close friend could be let in too to experience the faux freedom.

"Aw man, we love Tyrell," the son of the house would say. "We gotta get him in. Let's go down and open up the screen door in the back."

What an honor.

"Damn, Darius is super-cool. Maybe when you two leave, let him know he can come through," said the prince of bonfires.

The experience taught me that to access this world, I'd literally have to take the back door, and if there were any other Black people they could do so one or two at a time. That separatism can become self-propagating. I sometimes thought that I had to close the back door once inside. In my loneliest moments, I wore my badge as the token Black person with pride. I was never lost enough to think I *was* white. I didn't even want to be. But at my worst, I let myself slide into competing with other clever, charismatic Black kids who came into "my" space. Because I knew it wasn't truly my space. I was barely a guest and I felt replaceable.

I should mention the one time we brought a Black *girl* who was a friend of ours along to a bonfire house party. She was accused of stealing a purse and summarily kicked out. We left with her, but learned later the purse was found "hiding" behind the couch. Too late. The reputational damage had been done. She was never invited back for another bonfire house party and lies spread quickly at school about her alleged sticky fingers.

◆ ◆

Several of the people I spoke to in this book calculated, as kids, that their best chance of avoiding tragedy was to isolate themselves from other Black kids. Groups of Black teenagers are often seen as threatening, I assume because of gang stereotypes perpetuated in the media, which can lead to tension with police and other armed members of society. In my childhood I stumbled as I tried to balance staying close enough to my friends to maintain our bond while keeping enough distance to get by. When, as a teenager, I got a driver's license, it created a new threat: too many friends in the car was dangerous for all of us. Police and stereotyping drivers on the road could see me and my friends as a gang or troublemakers if we crammed into the car together as high schoolers are likely to do.

One day, the same year that my basketball team went to States, my dad texted me on my Nokia flip phone during third period to tell me to come out to the school parking lot at lunch. When I walked out, he pulled up in my parents' old 1994 gray Volvo. My dad handed me the keys. This was a handoff I'd been waiting for. I thought a car meant new freedom.

"Happy birthday," he said, glowing. "Check out the mats."

He had taken the car to a detailing shop where they'd engraved my name on the floor mats. They had also installed a Bose sound system. We hugged. This was a father-son celebration many boys like me don't get to have. I was so grateful, and elated. And then came gravity.

"So listen carefully," he said. "One passenger in the car at a time. No hats or du rags in here for anyone. Anybody who gets in, you check their pockets to make sure they're not carrying anything that's gonna get you arrested. Keep the music low, okay? We don't want any reason for the cops to pull you over."

I nodded. These were new rules to add to the set I received when we first moved into the cul-de-sac.

"Do you understand?" He wanted to hear me say it.

"Yes, sir."

He kissed the top of my head. "Happy birthday. You earned this by keeping your grades up," he said.

My basketball teammates were walking out of school for lunch. They noticed me and my dad in the gray Volvo.

"Scout!" they yelled. They ran over to high-five my dad.

Scout was their nickname for him because of the way he watched all of our games and our practices, sometimes taking notes like a college basketball scout.

"Boulder, is this yours?"

Boulder was their nickname for me because my head was too big for my 125-pound body.

"This thing looks like a hearse."

And so that was their nickname for my car: the hearse. My '94 Volvo, that never drove over the speed limit or carried more than one passenger at a time. My friends got so used to emptying their pockets before hopping in that they'd roll their eyes and turn their pockets inside out as soon as I pulled up in their driveways.

My dad only had to tell me the car rules once. I knew these rules were meant to avoid more than traffic tickets. They were instituted to try to avoid being unjustly arrested or killed by the police. Even these moments of love, gratitude, and celebration came with a survival warning for us as a Black family. We didn't talk about the long-lasting psychological effects of racial profiling or how we were going to rah-rah-sis-boom-bah, tweet, and hashtag the system until it changed. Nah. This was 2005. Just occasionally a reminder to "Take that hat off boy. They're gonna' think you're a thug." My dad was trying to keep me alive. I trusted him, because at that point he'd had a sixteen-year track record of doing so. Even when I saw my white friends packing six people into small vehicles, drinking in the car, blasting loud music, and doing donuts in our high school parking lot, I knew there was a separate set of rules for me, and my dad hardly had to remind me of that.

So most of the time, when my friends would pile into one of the "cooler" cars and blast music, or roll a J in the backseat, speeding to a local party, I'd chug along in my little Volvo alone at thirty-five miles per hour with the music at a laughably low volume until I showed up to the party a half an hour later. I continue to follow Dad's rules of driving to this day. Like all of my father's rules, they're hardly driving rules at all—they're rules to survive.

Once I drove a friend to a big football game at our school, and after the game, a few of my teammates and I were walking up the big hill from our school's football stadium to the main parking lot, alongside a hundred other rowdy high schoolers. Our football team had just been demolished in a blowout by our upcounty rival, Sherwood. There was an electricity in the air from the loud crack of bashing helmets and bruising hard hits we'd witnessed on the field. Everyone was restless. At once, the kids around us started running up the hill. My friend and I joined in. Hundreds of us flooded the parking lot. Fights broke out like little wildfires, the result of tensions over cheating boyfriends and girlfriends, neighborhood rivalries that had been bubbling for weeks, Jordans stepped on.

Violence routinely followed football games at our suburban high school that year, and the school quadrupled its police presence in response. But there were so many rambunctious teenagers in the lot that night. Those of us who weren't fighting gawked from the corners. Occasionally we'd pull a friend out of the fray. We huddled together, trying to look tough enough to avoid becoming targets.

Then the police on hand started grabbing Black boys and tossing them into squad cars. Most, like my friend, Terrence, weren't arrested. The police just drove them away from the lot and released them down the street to try to clear the crowd.

I watched the white kids scatter quickly to their cars and their parents' cars to get the hell away, but I didn't move. Me and my boys weren't hard by any stretch of the imagination, but we knew we were *supposed* to join the crowd of Black kids, even if only as spectators. To leave, while other friends stayed near the violence, would be an unforgivable abandonment. And we'd pay for it later by being called a punk, a bitch, or an oreo—Black on the outside, white on the inside. So we stayed planted—ten toes down as we call it today.

I followed the crowd as it moved to the front of our school building. Two rival groups of Black teenage girls, maybe four or five in each squad, collided. There was whooping and hollering from the watching crowd—so loud it drowned out the police sirens behind us. The fight was quick and vicious. A few punches thrown. Then the biggest girl appeared to grab another girl wearing a green hoodie, pulling her into what looked like a hug. The girl in the green hoodie dropped to the ground. The two groups sprinted away in different directions.

We watched the girl in the green hoodie shake for a beat on the pavement.

I took off running in another direction.

It didn't click that I'd just seen a stabbing. Later, a rumor spread that a van carrying one of the groups of teenage girls ran over the girl in the green hoodie, before speeding out of the lot to escape police. That bit was missing from the *Washington Post* story that covered the event on September 25, 2005.

I don't remember anything about the actual football game, or the parties we went to after we emptied out of the lot that night. But I remember what happened in the lot very clearly. Even in our middle-class suburb of Washington, DC, fights were common enough around Black kids that nothing I saw that night struck me as noteworthy. I didn't even tell my parents.

That night only became noteworthy when word got around that the victim had died and several of the girls involved were going to trial. Me and my Black classmates had watched a murder. We were watching a high school football game and then we had seen someone killed. As simple as that. There was no warning that something terrible was going to happen so quickly. We were at school, a place where we were meant to feel safe.

When my high school friends and I talk about that night, we also talk about the fact that we went to school the next day as though nothing had happened. But we must have been in distress, and ignored it. Right? How else does such close proximity to violence as children affect us? Does it make us strong, so that life's unpredictable and traumatic events don't unnerve and destroy us? I'd say so. Does it give us the perspective to know at an early age that life is fleeting, and that any day can be our last, so we have to live for the moment? I'd say so. Does it give us a sense of humor to see the irony that something as seemingly harmless as a high school sporting event can turn into a crime scene in seconds? I'd say so. I need to believe it gives us the detachment and perspective and strength we need to move forward through chaos and pain without becoming shell-shocked and paralyzed by grief.

Because otherwise, it's just too unfair.

Here's what the *Washington Post* story didn't say, either. Here's what no one said that night—not the people in the crowd, or the school officials, or the police:

One student got to jump in a car with four friends, blast the radio, speed out of the lot, and go hang out by a bonfire. Another student was stabbed, then run over by a car, then taken away on a gurney.

The differentiating factor was melanin. Race.

I need to believe there's a deeper purpose in what we endure in the so-called safety of our schools—even in affluent school districts like mine—where our classmates, beginning in preschool, call us names, bully us, and marginalize us in classroom discussions, and where our friends can be arrested and stabbed and killed. Because if there isn't a deeper purpose in all of this, what's the point of learning? What's the point in living?

JEWEL BURKS SOLOMON

"I had a conversation with a Black investor and he said, 'You're not going to be able to raise money with the team that you have currently.' He was like, 'You just can't. It's not gonna happen. You need to find a white man to do this with you.'"

Jewel Burks Solomon currently serves as head of Google for start-ups in the US, where she works to level the playing field for underrepresented startup founders and communities. Additionally, she is a managing partner at Collab Capital, an investment fund to connect Black founders to the financial and social capital they need to build profitable, sustainable businesses.

From 2013 to 2016 Jewel was CEO and cofounder of Partpic, a startup that was acquired by Amazon and which streamlined the purchase of maintenance and repair parts using computer vision. Before founding Partpic, Jewel served in management, enterprise sales, and strategic diversity roles at McMaster-Carr Supply Company and Google Inc. Jewel is a native of Nashville, Tennessee, and a graduate of Howard University. She is a member of the 2019 Class of Henry Crown Fellows within the Aspen Global Leadership Network at the Aspen Institute. Jewel is an advocate for representation in and access to the technology industry.

Jewel is almost six feet tall. She has a thick Black Southern accent. She can't hide or blend in around white people. But I was surprised to hear Jewel describe the overt racism she experienced while raising money for her tech startup. I knew, of course, that microaggressions and subtle racism were prevalent in the venture capital space, but I was floored by the boldfaced racism Jewel encountered in her fundraising journey. A venture capitalist told Jewel plainly that to get cash to build Partpic, Jewel would have to add white people to her team.

Jewel was used to facing a racial gap in every professional and academic setting. A grade school teacher told her mom Jewel would struggle once she was moved into gifted classes at a white school. Even as a child, Jewel used those low expectations as fuel. In our conversation she traced how those same low expectations follow her at every stop of her career, but she keeps pushing through them. Grace and persistence are Jewel's Black Magic. She doesn't explode when white people call her a diva and she doesn't stop going when someone questions her ability. She's nonstop. She just keeps building.

Chad: I'm going to pick a point in your story that stood out to me, and then we're gonna jump all over the place. I read one of your blog entries where you described fundraising for Partpic. You said people said you needed a non-Black person on your founding team to raise any venture capital money. Can you describe what happened there and what that meant to you? What did that do to you?

Jewel: Initially, what it looked like was people suggesting that I get a technical cofounder. When I first started, they didn't put a label on that person, like "This person needs to be a male" or "This person needs to be a white" or whatever. They just said, "You need to have a technical person that's doing this with you." So, I didn't really pursue any certain type of person, I just was looking for someone who had the technical skill set to help me. And it so happened that the people that I came upon or who expressed interest in working with me were Black people, for the most part.

When we started forming a team, the first technical folks that we got on board were Black people. The team was pretty much all Black for the first year or so. As I went to present Partpic to potential investors and share what the team looked like, that's when it started to become more clear. When people said "technical person" they were implying that I add "someone who is non-Black" or someone who is white or someone who is male. Those things started coming out more overtly. I had a conversation with a Black investor and he said, "You're not going to be able to raise money with the team that you have currently." He was like, "You just can't. It's not gonna happen. You need to find a white man to do this with you." In another investor meeting, an Asian woman who was a partner said something similar. It was me, her, and a white man who was the leader of her firm, and she asked the question "Is your team still Black?" following up from an earlier time that we'd met.

It wasn't even coded. She was saying: this is something I need to know as a determining factor of whether or not I'm going to invest in the company. And from her perspective, I think she felt that as a minority, she could ask that. I don't know if it was something they had previously discussed or not.

And then, it came out all the time whenever I was in meetings. I could see the looks on people's faces when we put our team slide up and the faces on the team slide were all Black. So, it happened in both pretty direct ways, where people were questioning me, "Why does the team look like this?" And then every time I expanded and grew the company, the questions became a little bit more subtle.

Chad: Woah, okay, let me back up. What was your life like growing up in Tennessee? Did you ever feel like you had to be more than one person, racially? Did you ever feel like you had to take on more than one racial identity to try to fit in?

Jewel: Yes. I was born in Mobile, Alabama, which is a pretty segregated place, even to this day. I grew up primarily in Nashville, Tennessee. I grew up in majority white schools. I went to public school, but from sixth grade until I finished high school, I was in academic magnet schools, and those have lottery systems for admissions. They filtered out a lot of the minority students, so most of the time I was with majority white classmates.

I was definitely a high achiever, starting in fifth grade. In the fifth grade I remember thinking *I have to be more.* It was actually spurred by a comment my fifth-grade teacher made to my mom. I was there.

My mom took me to introduce me to the teacher before school started. My mom said, "You know, Jewel is a really great student and she's going to do well in your class." And the teacher said, "Well, let's not get ahead of ourselves. This is a really difficult school. Let's be prepared that maybe she won't do so well."

I took that as a challenge. From that point on I had a chip on my shoulder. From that point on I always assumed I had to do more to prove people wrong. And that carried on, all the way through high school. And then it broke a little bit when I was in college, because I made the decision to go to an HBCU. Then I didn't feel so much like everything I was doing was to prove myself among all these white people.

But yes, my teacher's comment made me think, *Oh, I have to be better and maybe I have to be a different me in a school setting with all these white folks versus who I am at home or at church or in my extracurricular activities.*

Chad: What did it look like trying to prove yourself or fit in with white people growing up? Can you give material examples? Was it the way that you talked? Was it the way that you dressed? Was it the way that you carried yourself? Who you dated?

Jewel: It started in elementary school. I actually forgot about this. In elementary school, my grandmother was the assistant principal, and then my fourth-grade year, she was the principal. That created this friction between me and the Black kids that went to my elementary school. This notion of "not being Black enough" started in my head. I was definitely the teacher's pet. I didn't live in the same neighborhood that the rest of the Black kids came from, because they were bussed from a certain area. I was just in that school because my grandmother had gotten me into it and she was the principal.

So, when I was in elementary school, even though there was a small population of Black kids at that school, I was always pretty much alienated from those kids. And that's where the conversation about "Oh, she thinks she's better, she thinks she's white, she talks different," all these types of things came up. But at the same time, I was not really fitting in with the white kids because I didn't look like them, by any means. I was on the soccer team, and all the other girls were white, and that's when questions about "Well, what's wrong with your hair?" and "Where's your dad?" would come up. Those types of questions started to make me question a lot of things, and make me realize that I was very different.

Chad: What did you do to prove yourself, besides academic achievement? How did you change yourself to fit in, depending on who was around you?

Jewel: I think I turned inward. I was the kid in school who knew everyone and everybody knew me. But it was because they knew me as the teacher's pet or the girl who gets the awards at the academic ceremonies and not because I was the one who was the class clown or the life of the party. That made me shy in social situations. I had maybe one or two close friends, but I wasn't close to a lot of people. I was just good at what I was good at, but outside of that I was pretty much just doing my own thing. Personality-wise, I put all my attention toward achieving and not really toward making people like me or not like me, because I felt like that was too much of a challenge.

Chad: How old were you when you started to consciously turn yourself inward?

Jewel: It started in elementary school when I felt rejected by the Black kids and the white kids. I really didn't feel like I had one friend who was in my same boat.

In middle school most of the kids were in the same boat, where they tested out of their particular elementary schools, and so we were more equal, in terms of all wanting to do well academically. So I was able to connect with more people, but I still had already kind of formulated this focus: I go to school to do good in school. That's my thing. That's what I thrive on.

I get awards and that's my life. And yeah, I think that pretty much stuck with me. And it started in elementary school.

Chad: And, it sounds like you were in a place where you were around Black people often. You were around white people often. Neither one of those two groups, at least as far as you could tell, looked at you as fully a part of those groups. And you didn't really see yourself as fully part of those groups at that time. Is that fair to say?

Jewel: Yeah. I guess the other things that I didn't mention—when I was in elementary and middle school, I had really, really long hair. I remember that being a topic of discussion. I remember girls would threaten to cut my hair off. I ran track and I remember that was always a thing. We're lining up to run, and girls would talk about how they're gonna cut my hair out.

Chad: Black girls? White girls?

Jewel: Black girls, yeah.

Chad: Mmhmm.

Jewel: My mom was very—well, is—very pro-Black for sure. So the education I was getting at home was, like, I had the anthology of all these books by Booker T. Washington and W. E. B. DuBois. My only toy I had growing up was this African-American trivia game. So, that was my idea of fun. Whenever my mom's friends would come over, I'd challenge them to this trivia game that was all about Black history. So I wasn't confused about "Am I Black?" or "Am I Black enough?" because I was getting that type of education at home. That was enough for me.

Chad: Right. But it was when you went out into the world that other people brought their own judgment about whether or not you were Black enough.

Jewel: Yeah. And that came from what I looked like. How I spoke. Where I lived at the time. All of those things were factors in people trying to figure out what it was all about as it relates to being Black or not being Black or whatever.

Chad: So what about your college experience? I know that you went to Howard. You were in DC, which is a predominantly Black city, or was at that time. You probably were surrounded by Black people. What parts of you did you carry with you to Howard? How did that environment affect you once you were there?

Jewel: When I got to Howard I felt like, "Oh my gosh, I can breathe." It felt like most of the people there had a similar experience. They grew up always in between multiple worlds, and it's like they chose to come to Howard because they just needed a break from that. They want to be in an environment where they can just learn and grow into who they are and meet other people that have a like mind. Or maybe meet people who have a totally different mindset, but at least the thing about race isn't always looming.

From the moment I stepped on campus, I was like, "Man." First of all, I feel so great knowing that I'm not the only one. All these people were killing it wherever they came from, and they also caused me to really feel more confident about my skills and who I am. I felt like if I could still compete with this group of people coming from all over the place, then I really am smart. I do have what it takes, or whatever.

I definitely think Howard gave me a chance to breathe a bit. It instilled sort of the same things that my mom had worked on. It just really gave me a foundation in understanding my history and meeting other really, really smart and talented Black people, connecting with alumni and making connections in DC.

When I got to Howard I was in the School of Business. My main focus was getting internships. For my freshman year, it was pretty much a competition to see which students would get internships at Goldman Sachs. And so that was my main focus. I want to intern at Goldman. The school is kind of pushing students to go to Wall Street, and so I thought, *Okay, this is what I need to do.*

I got the Goldman internship and then this whole thing about being the minority comes back into play because there weren't many Black interns. I went back into "I must prove myself" mode. But at least this time I had more confidence coming from the position of "Well I won this internship from all the other students that could have been chosen." When I got into Goldman, I don't know if it was more so about being Black or more so about being from the South, but I felt like I had to really pick up the pace. That summer, I really picked up the pace of life.

One particular thing that happened: a woman who I was working for asked me a question, or she asked me to do something. In my response I used the term "right quick." And I didn't know that that wasn't typical language.

Chad: You said what?

Jewel: I said "right quick."

Chad: Oh, okay.

Jewel: Apparently that's not something that everyone says. I didn't know that at the time. She cracked up. She could not stop laughing. Honestly, I had no idea. That's just one example of where I was like, "Oh, I need to put on my white . . ." you know, whatever. I was coming from Nashville with my little Southern drawl. That wasn't acceptable in that particular environment.

Chad: You said, "I felt like I needed to put on my white . . . you know, 'blank,' whatever." What is the "blank"? Your white . . . what?

Jewel: I don't wanna say "voice," because I don't believe the whole notion that, like, white people talk right and Black people talk . . . whatever. But more so that I just could not necessarily come as my full self. In my mind, at that point in time, the thing that came out of my mouth that I say was "right quick." And I felt like that was the correct answer to her question. But that experience made me put up a barrier. Or a filter, I guess. Between what ordinarily would come out of my mouth or what I would ordinarily do, and what I perceived to be the correct thing to do in the presence of these people that I was working with. So, maybe it's not a white thing, maybe it's a corporate filter. There were several experiences where whatever my nature told me to do, I couldn't do at the time.

Chad: What are the consequences if you don't restructure the way that you speak or the way that you approach people in those environments? Like, what does it cost you?

Jewel: In that internship, my main goal was "I need to get a returning offer." So everything I was doing, I'm thinking, *How is this going to come off?* and *Is this gonna be perceived well or not perceived well?* Because at the end of the day I need these people to give me a recommendation so that I can come back. I think it just made me examine—and really second-guess—every single thing that I did to make sure that it would be perceived well to the people that I was counting on to recommend me to come back.

Chad: And in those moments, how much of your mind were you using to make sure that you used the "right" inflections and the "right" social cues? And how much of your mind were you using to do the actual work?

Jewel: My presentation and social cues took up more than 50 percent of my mind. At every moment I was thinking, *Is this the right thing to do? Is it the right thing to do? What do I remember seeing this other person that seems to be in a good position doing?* Because at that time, I just didn't have enough experience. So, I was really kind of learning on the fly. I did identify a few Black women right when I got there who I felt like, *Okay, they seem to be well respected. They seem to have it together. I'll look and see what they're doing and try to do that. And hopefully the others will accept me the way they seem to have accepted these women.*

Chad: You have now worked at several corporations. You've run your own company. How important is it that you know the social cues and you're able to turn them on when you're around colleagues? How important is that for your work, and what impact does that have on your work today?

Jewel: It's super-important. Going back to what I mentioned about my upbringing and my childhood, that's one area where I've always felt unsure. And so I've focused, even in my work, on making sure that whatever work I'm producing is so great that I don't have to interact with people socially. It's a crutch. Socializing is required, especially when I need to fundraise and kind of schmooze and all that stuff. But that's not my comfort zone, so I've always tried to make it so that people are talking about my work versus how much they enjoy me, personally. I do think social interactions are very important, but I have never really felt like, 100 percent comfortable in that.

Chad: It sounds like you've learned so much about line-straddling from growing up in a very pro-Black household then going to very racially mixed schools then going to an HCBU and then working at huge companies like Google and Amazon. What from those experiences are you using to your advantage? Is there anything from those experiences that you've wanted to let go—but haven't been able to?

Jewel: The biggest thing I learned when I was at Google was that people seemed to be more concerned with experiences versus race. When I first got to Google, people were always talking about their vacations and where they traveled. Lucky for me, when I was growing up, I had opportunities to travel because of my mom's job. She was an insurance sales agent and did pretty well in her career, so we were able to take a trip pretty much every year.

So often at work, I remember thinking I couldn't relate to certain conversations, but if someone started talking about their vacation to Italy, I could jump in. I could connect with them and get in on that particular topic. I realized that if you engage in those conversations, then people start to let walls down a bit and say, "Oh, well this person at least is on my level when it comes to their travel experiences or whatever."

I guess the lesson was to try to connect with people based on experiences versus "oh, this person looks like me," which I think is by nature what feels better to do. But in a situation where you're really the only Black person on the team, you can't do that. So today, when I'm put in situations where I'm trying to connect with people, I try to think about shared experiences. What are places that we've gone? What are the things we can connect on?

Chad: Is that something that you learned as a kid? Or is that something that you learned as an adult? 'Cause I wanna focus in on some things that you learned from that experience line-jumping, growing up, that eventually made you turn inward, to use your words. Is there anything that you learned from those experiences as a young person that you are now applying in your professional life?

Jewel: I see it as a necessity in corporate America to play into their—and by "their," I mean white people's, 'cause primarily they run a lot of corporations—but to kind of play into their way, if you will. There are so many discussions about this whole notion about bringing your whole self to work and being authentic and all that stuff. There's much discussion about it, but especially in more conservative companies, I still feel like it's very necessary to play the line.

Chad: Is there anything else that you wanted to get in while we are here?

Jewel: I want to talk about being a woman and being a Black woman. I never know which one is hurting me more in my everyday encounters and when people approach me in the business world. I don't know which is affecting their judgments more or how they're going to interact with me. I think about that. I remember in our Partpic pitches, I always thought, *Should I be downplaying the fact that I'm a woman? Or should I be playing into that because most of the audiences I'm presenting in front of are men?*

Chad: How do you separate—if you can separate—your experience and your struggle as a Black person from your experience and struggle as a woman? Do you separate those things? Where do they sit in your mind?

Jewel: It's very difficult to de-couple those two things because the way people perceive Black women, I feel, is very specific. If I were a Black man I would be experiencing something different. If I was a white woman I would be experiencing something different. A lot of the feedback I've gotten—especially in dealing with investors—was very specific to me being a Black woman. And I don't really know how I could possibly parse those two things. I kind of gave up trying. But I always think about it: *Are they doing that because I'm a woman or because I'm Black?* But usually I feel like people have a specific idea about Black women. If I reinforce their ideas, then they're going to treat me one way. If I come into conflict with their ideas, they're going to treat me another way. So. Yeah.

Chad: In moments of tension, or moments when you feel the most persecuted or judged or disrespected or overlooked, what version of yourself comes out? We all have these different sides to us.

Jewel: I think it depends on what part of me is being attacked. I got feedback from people that there was a notion going around that I am a diva. That was a thread going around when investors talked about our company, Partpic. Something that would come up is "Jewel is a diva." I took offense to that, personally. But I try to take my personal feelings out of it and understand. Okay, if this is what people think, how are they taking that out on my company? How is that affecting our impact and what decisions they're making in relation to my company? If I find that way of thinking does impact how people are dealing with my company, then of course I would try to correct the situation. I would try to use humility as a tool to get people to back down from that notion.

Obviously, initially when I heard people were calling me a diva, I was defensive. I didn't like it and it still doesn't make me happy, but I guess when I heard it a second time I was more so inquisitive and reflective. I thought about when someone would have made that assumption or judgment. I thought about how they could feel that so deeply that they wanted to tell other people. Most of the time when I hear things, I try to determine the impact on my business and then I'll deal with my own personal feelings about it later.

Maybe when that person spoke with me, my response to his or her disbelief in my company was assertive. And maybe when that person comes into contact with assertive Black women, he or she categorizes them as divas. So maybe they put me in that category too. But it could just be that I had different opinions than them or I said whatever I said in a way that he or she stereotyped. But that's their problem. It's not for me.

BRIAN SHIELDS

"I didn't fully realize what being 'Black' meant until one of my teachers in the third grade pulled me aside to make sure the other kids weren't taking advantage of me because I was the smart kid in class and the only Black kid in class."

Brian is an entrepreneur and investor. He is currently co-owner and the president of Hill & Co. Property Management, a real estate company. Formerly, Brian was vice president of business development at Mynd, a VC-backed property management company, where he led growth from five hundred to eight thousand plus properties under management. Before that, Brian was head of business development at Funding Circle, a peer-to-peer lending marketplace which IPO-ed in 2018 and is a publicly traded company. He began his career in investment banking and private equity at Barclays (formerly Lehman Brothers) and Welsh, Carson, Anderson and Stowe. Brian earned his BA in Business Administration from Morehouse College.

As a sophomore, I met Brian on one of his many returning trips to help students at Morehouse prepare for job interviews.

I knew Brian's father was Black and his mother was Filipino. I expected Brian to share a balance of his experiences growing up as a Black man and his experiences growing up as an Asian man. Instead, Brian dug into his process of racial reckoning as a grade school student, seeking acceptance from kids who didn't know how to place him racially.

Brian seemed optimistic, even as a kid, that if he exposed himself to failure—as he attempted to make friends across races—he would eventually find a community. Brian applied that lesson in his career by taking risks as an entrepreneur to grow his businesses. Risk-taking is the Black Magic Brian honed growing up as a biracial kid in Texas. As Brian points out, Superman didn't know he was Superman when he was a kid. He needed trial and error to realize his superpowers. So do we.

———

Chad: How did you grow up?

Brian: I was born in Huntsville, Texas, but for all intents and purposes I grew up in Houston, Texas. I am the child of an immigrant from the Philippines and a very blue-collar Southern Black man.

I spent a good chunk of my early years in Huntsville, which is a town of about twenty thousand people. My father was the kind of guy who everybody around town knew. You know, he'd walk down the street—"Hey, Joe!" He'd walk into a store— "Hey, Joe!" And I became "Joe Boy's son."

People held my father up as this magnanimous person who was highly sociable and well liked, but he was very emotionally distant, so I didn't know him very well. He would come home, work, go through his routine, but not really engage with me. He wasn't the type to come to my sports games or my practices or speeches or whatever. And then separately, my mom, who was a Filipino immigrant, had a very strong educational desire for me and wanted me to be exposed to the world. Part of that was because exposure and pursuit of education and opportunity gave her the chance to leave the Philippines and get a really great-paying job and create opportunities for the rest of her family. My mom is the oldest of eight, so she would pay for people in our family to go to school and learn medicine and things like that.

My mom worked nights, so during the day I would be home by myself or with my dad, who was doing his own thing. So I would be independent, with a lot of space to do *my* own thing. That was great. Over time I developed into a person who was really comfortable in my independence.

I figured out what to do. I made friends. I found activities I wanted to do with the local kids and played basketball and rode bikes or whatever. And then I shaped my after-school activities like karate or piano lessons. Eventually, I got into things like wrestling and competitive video games. So that independence was a foundational part of my life. Just shaping the things I wanted to do without a lot of guidance and then setting a path to go get into those things. And then living with the successes or consequences of those decisions.

Separately, growing up as a mixed kid was really very enriching. There was a phase where I didn't understand what "race" was. I just spent most of my time with my mom and she didn't have the full context of race in America. But she kind of understood it. I didn't fully realize what being "Black" meant until one of my teachers in the third grade pulled me aside to make sure the other kids weren't taking advantage of me because I was the smart kid in class and the only Black kid in class. So I didn't understand what that meant until I got older. But then, you know, everybody has those experiences like the first time somebody called them the n-word. Or people treat you differently because they feel threatened by a ten-year-old or a thirteen-year-old Black kid being around them. Or, you know, the first and ongoing interactions with the police as we get older. All those things remind you that you are a person of color in this country and that the rules are slightly different.

But then, having this foundation in another culture also made me feel one-foot-in-one-foot-out because my Black friends would treat me differently because I have an Asian mom. So there would be different kinds of jokes. Or I wouldn't even understand the context of some of the things they were saying 'cause I didn't grow up like them. I think that made me really good at being able to connect and be with various kinds of people. I had such a different background and it forced me to be in tune with a lot of people.

I think about my time in Texas as foundationally creating this competitive aspect of myself. I knew I was good at stuff—academically and athletically—and I wanted to structure my time in a way that helped me get better at doing whatever it is I decided to do. I had this multifaceted social experience where I didn't have siblings, so I had to go outside the house to find people to connect with and peers to shape me. I couldn't fit into anybody's easy box in Texas, and I had to find ways to just connect with people and overcome that. People would be like, "Oh, here's this Black and Asian kid. I don't really get it. You got good hair. I don't really get it."

So then the white kids didn't really know how to treat me and the Black kids didn't really know how to treat me and the Asian kids didn't really know how to treat me. So, I just said, "You know, I'm gonna show y'all. I'm gonna be friends with all of y'all. I'm going to figure out how to speak y'all's language." I wanted to bring everybody together to connect over partying or school or projects. I just wanted to get people in the room and make them feel safe and help us work together.

I took that with me to college. I went to Morehouse College—class of 2006. It was definitely one of the most important, consequential, and best decisions I've ever made in my life.

And it was totally not my decision, directly. I didn't know what Morehouse *was* until I was a senior in high school applying to schools and my counselor pulled me aside and said, "Listen, you need to apply to Morehouse," and I was like, "I don't know what that is." She told me her daughter was going to Spelman and I should be considering Morehouse because it was really good for Black men.

My first reaction was "I don't wanna go to no Black school, that's stupid." I thought that would limit my opportunities. Discovering what it meant to be a Black man in America was a journey for me. So I applied, got a full scholarship, and as a very cost-conscious person, I decided I was going to Morehouse. That is just a testament to providence and the existence of God because that was not any doing on my part. It wasn't like, "I'm a self-made person, I know what I'm gonna do." That's all BS. I think people who say that forget the fact that there are outside forces that help you and help people help you get to where you wanna be. I definitely believe that's what got me to Morehouse.

So Morehouse came and went, and I think one of the big lessons I took away from that experience was knowing what it felt like to be a Black man, but not be defined by being a Black man. You look out at Morehouse and you have three thousand Black men and they're all different. You have nerds, jocks, people coming from privileged backgrounds, people who come from the exact opposite backgrounds. All of them are there, and the one common thread we all have is we used to be the Black dude in class or on the sports team or whatever. Now we're just the jock, the nerd, the wealthy dude, the non-wealthy dude. And that component of race comes away. That was super-powerful for me as I evolved at school, because it gave me foundational confidence in who I am.

As I emerged from that into the rest of the world, I felt confidence that I didn't have to carry the narrative of "You gotta do right because you're this Black man. You gotta do right because everybody's looking at you" running in my head. It was more like, "I know I can do right."

Chad: When I was twenty-three I had this moment where I realized, "Oh, shit. I'm in this corporate environment. I'm Black. That is gonna hold me back. How can I solve this puzzle to flip this in my favor?" What would you say to someone trying to solve a similar puzzle?

Brian: Look, I think it somewhat depends on the context, right? Like if you're a line guy at Delta, that's different than if you're in Hollywood, or even a tech company. One of the things I learned at Morehouse, and that I've learned in my career, is that being a person of color is actually advantageous, for many different reasons. Two really facetious but helpful reasons are: Everybody remembers you, you know? If you are the only Black person or brown person in a company, they're always going to know who you are. That can be intimidating, but if you do something productive and tell people, they'll tell people. They'll be like, "I know Brian" or "I know Chad, yeah." It makes networking super-easy.

So, that's facetious, but in reality you have a different perspective than a lot of other people. One thing I've had to learn throughout my career is that there are things that I see that other people might not be aware of because they just don't have the gifts and experiences that I've had. I would say, trust that in yourself, because you have experiences that are different from people in the room. Or from me. And that is critical in making you an individual, but also in giving you some ability to see something somebody else hasn't seen. That is valuable in a conversation. Trust that. Pass that and play with it, because you're not going to figure it out day one. But if you just trust that you have something unique to give the world, and that you just need to keep searching and trying different things, eventually you'll find it. And when you find it, you'll do it. This is great.

Superman didn't figure out he was Superman the minute he was born you know? It took a whole process for him to get out of Smallville and learn that he can fly. And then eventually he's Superman. Go be Black Superman.

DERAY MCKESSON

"I want Black people to understand that Blackness is its own sort of power and it's not only important in reference to other things. Our power does not lie solely in the fact that we've overcome trauma. Our power lies in the fact that we created in the midst of trauma."

DeRay is a civil rights activist, author, public speaker, educator, teacher, and school system leader and one of the leaders of the Black Lives Matter movement. In 2015, he was named one of the World's 50 Greatest Leaders by *Fortune* magazine. DeRay earned his BA in Government and Legal Studies from Bowdoin College and holds honorary doctorates from the Maryland Institute College of Art and the New School.

When DeRay answered the phone for our interview, I heard exhaustion in his voice. He's been traveling nonstop for nearly four years, protesting against police brutality and other racial injustices. He recently faced accusations of using tragedy to build his personal brand and line his pockets with movement funds. (He denied those allegations.) He lives under the magnifying glass of public scrutiny because of his work at the forefront of activism and his recognizable image, including his unmistakable blue Patagonia vest which he, apparently, hasn't washed or replaced in years.

But what stayed with me from our conversation was not his significant achievements, or the accusations, but a simple idea: DeRay said he only realized as a sixth grader, when a teacher wrote something incorrect on a board, that white people could be wrong. It shocked me that someone with such a clear and independent way of thinking and speaking on racial matters lived under the impression that white people were always right until he was nearly a teenager. I shouldn't have been so struck. That idea—*white people can be wrong*—seems so obvious but can be so easy to overlook as a Black person in this country. Most authority figures are white. Presidents. CEOs. Coaches. Teachers. Media members. Sometimes I still forget to question the white faces on the news.

As a teacher, DeRay encourages his students to challenge him and think for themselves, never mind his authority. DeRay believes Blackness to be its own form of power and magic, but I believe DeRay's specific form of Black Magic is his boldness as a free thinker, a conviction in his belief that Black people deserve equality as a human right. That conviction puts him in harm's way—often in handcuffs or inches away from potentially deadly police actions. But that conviction has also inspired millions to protest against racism all over the world.

––––––––

Chad: How did you grow up, DeRay?

DeRay: My mother left when I was three, but both of my parents were addicted to drugs and my father entered recovery and my mother didn't. My mother and father jointly raised us until middle school, then it was just my father and me and my sister. My sister's name is TeRay and she is a year and a half older.

Chad: When did you become consciously aware of your Blackness?

DeRay: I grew up in an all-Black community, and in sixth grade my father moved us to a different neighborhood so we could be zoned in different schools. He put us in Baltimore County. That was the first time I'd ever really been around white people and certainly the first time I'd had white teachers. And that was the first time I understood both Blackness and whiteness as cultural elements and not simply as skin tones. I knew our churches were different, but I didn't have the language to express those differences. But it was in going to those schools as a sixth grader where I was like, "Oh this is not something as basic as skin tone. It's something cultural, something is culturally different here."

Chad: What seemed to be the application of those differences? Did you understand whiteness as an advantage at that age?

DeRay: I didn't have the language for it, but I remember not knowing white people could be wrong, because on TV white people were always right. I remember being a student in sixth grade when a white teacher put something wrong on the board and I was just like, "Wow." I remember the shock. So I understood disparities, because the community I grew up in and the community we moved to had such different resources.

The second way I saw the disparities was in the way we were tracked as students in high school. There was gifted and talented, which was the highest tier, and then there was honors and then there was standard. That's what the course tracks were called. Almost all of the Black students were in standard. I was in AP, which was the same thing as gifted and talented. And I remember being in AP Psychology and AP Government, and it was always two or three Black people. Even in Honors English, I was the only Black person. I remember thinking, *That's not fair*, but I didn't have the language for it as a sixth grader or a ninth grader. But I knew something was off.

Chad: In addition to your work in activism, you have a career in education. What is the responsibility of educators to help students in this country understand racial dynamics?

DeRay: I think that what the best teachers do is set up students with a set of skills that they can apply to a host of disciplines and a host of experiences with the knowledge base that allows them to be nimble. As a math teacher, we would have these word problems that were only about golf. I can't properly convey how many of the word problems were about golf. And most of my kids hadn't played golf. I didn't know how to play golf. So what is my responsibility to make this content actually applicable to my students' lives in a way that makes it accessible? I think that is one part of the educator's responsibilities. How do we make the content less abstract and more tangible so that students can understand and appreciate it?

My job as an educator is to make sure the students have the basic information so they can build on it. So, the way we teach history is important. When you think about the map that is used in the vast majority of classrooms in the country, it makes all the continents look proportionate in size when Africa is actually just much bigger than the rest of the continents [besides Asia]. We should teach the true history. We should teach the honest map of the way the world actually looks. So, I do think educators have a responsibility to students to teach content that is right and give them skills that allow them to do something with that content, to both analyze it and to make analyzing constructive.

Chad: I'm curious to know if you believe in the premise of this book. Do you think we can use the lessons we learn from Blackness to fight back against the ways we're disadvantaged by race?

DeRay: I wish I had so many things as a younger person. It wasn't until college that I understood Blackness as powerful outside of Civil Rights icons. As a young person, the most glorious ideas of Blackness that I had were the resistors in the Civil Rights Movement. I didn't have knowledge around Black art, I didn't have knowledge around the way Black people had used words as tools and weapons and shields. There's so many things I wish I had known earlier that would have, in hindsight, given me a boost of confidence and an understanding that I exist not in the shadow of those before me but in their glow.

I think about the one book that probably meant the most

to me as a young person: *The People Could Fly*. It was a young adult book written around a set of stories. In one of those stories, the Black people are flying as a metaphor for freedom and a host of other things. I remember that book because that was the first entrance that I ever had into thinking about Black people as otherworldly and magical and special in a really different way. So yeah, the premise of this book makes sense to me.

Chad: Then how do you apply Black Magic as an activist?

DeRay: What the best teachers do is walk into a classroom and know that the gifts already existed before they got there. Part of the work of great teaching is to remind students that the gift will always be there and show them how to access the gift both in my presence and when I'm gone. That is the best that I can do, is help you access this content and these skills right now and do it really well and do it far after you know me or see me. What the worst teachers do is make students believe that the gift only exists in the teacher's presence.

When I think about activism and organizing, the same applies. Part of what we do as activists in the community having conversations with people is tell them they actually have power. One of the ways the status quo plays musical chairs with itself is by convincing you that you don't have power or that the power only exists in these pockets. But what I'm here to tell you as an activist and an organizer is that you have a lot of power. You already have power and there's power in the way that we have overcome, there's power in the way that we think about joy and live joy. There's power in the way we shape culture. These are not insignificant ways to move about the world, and that is what I can do as an activist.

So, when I think about the overall message, that's what I'm always trying to convey to people. That is the root of activism. That is the root of organizing, and it shows up in a host of places. It shows up in high school classrooms. I'm an adult and I'll go into classrooms and young people challenge me and I want you to know that you can challenge me. I guess I've done this work longer than you because I've been alive longer than you, but I want you to know that the way you think about things in the world is valid and we should go back and forth about it and you should push.

I want Black people to understand that Blackness is its own sort of power and it's not only important in reference to other things. Our power does not lie solely in the fact that we've overcome trauma. Our power lies in the fact that we created in the midst of trauma. We have understood the power of joy and how joy can be liberatory. That is a part of our power that is unique to Blackness. That's my long answer to a short question.

Chad: Why do you think you are a leader of a movement? Why do you think you specifically were born and lived and eventually became this person at this moment?

DeRay: You know, I don't spend much time thinking about the "why." I'm so deeply mired in the work that I'm just trying to stay focused. When I think about this, there are a couple things that come to mind. One is that I'm proud to be one of the many people who are trying to do good work. So, when I think about what it means to lead, I know that people are leading in ways that are seemingly big and small all across the country. So, that's the first thing.

The best leaders help people go places they don't think they can go or should go while helping them feel safe in the travel and create new space as they travel. When I was in the street in Ferguson, I started a newsletter. I used Twitter as a way to mobilize people and organize people in partnership with so many other people. That was about streamlining and being as strategic as we could be and creating as much space for people to do as much good work as possible. And that was the focus when I was invited to other cities to help out. "How can I use my platform to help you to do the best work that you possibly can do?" And when I think about the policy work that we've done and the data work that we've done, it's like, how can we put as much of this into the public space as possible? So that people can use it and do great things with it. And sometimes they'll do the great things with us and sometimes they'll do the great things without us, but we will have at least contributed the content so that activists and organizers and people in the community don't have to search anymore. We will have done that work for them.

Chad: Considering those people in the community, let's say this book comes out and some Black kid, late teens/early twenties, picks it up because they want to understand their own Black Magic. What would you tell them to help them understand their intrinsic power?

DeRay: When we say the system is broken, people often reply and say that it's not broken, it was designed to be this way. My takeaway is always that it was designed. And because it was designed, we can design something else. Because it was built, we can build something else. When I was a young person, I thought the world just was. As an adult, I realize somebody just made that up. Like, what is a crime? A crime is just action with a consequence. That's all it is, right? Somebody decided that that action should have a consequence, and we can make different decisions about what actions have consequences and what those consequences are. Somebody decided that houses look this way. Somebody decided that those five-year-olds weren't worthy of dinner tonight. These were all decisions that were made by things that we allow to happen.

There's an AIDS activist, her name is Dr. Krim. She always says we allowed AIDS to happen. She says that the energy that AIDS activists had to put in to get the first drugs to respond to the crisis took so much fighting and so long that it's like the government just allowed it to happen. It's like we could have made different choices. We could have gotten in front of it. We could have moved quicker. But some set of people didn't think that those early people who were impacted by AIDS were worthy enough of an intervention and we allowed that. It's like, we allow poverty. We allow certain crimes, by creating the conditions for them. And those are all things that are choices at the system level. I'm more and more empowered to believe and to understand that when we find our power, we can actually do things that people said were impossible.

Chapter Three

COLLEGE: HBCUS, PWIS, AND HIGHER LEARNING

"The function of education is to teach one to think intensively and to think critically. Intelligence plus character—that is the goal of true education."

—Dr. Martin Luther King, Jr.

━━━━━◆◆◆◆◆━━━━━

For four years, as a student at Morehouse College in Atlanta, I almost forgot white people existed. I mean, I knew they existed. I saw them on TV. I saw them on Facebook. I had a white professor once every other semester or so. I saw them at Lenox Mall and Chick-fil-A. But for long stretches—weeks, sometimes months—I never encountered a white person.

At Morehouse, nearly *everyone* was Black. My roommates were Black. My professors were Black. The chair of the honors program was Black. The cops on campus were Black. The custodial staff was Black. The cheerleaders were Black. The football team was Black (except for the kicker, he was Iranian). The Student Government Association was Black. The fraternities and sororities were all Black. The art kids, the science program, the deadbeats, the musicians, the dorm resident associates, the weed dealers, the barbers, the cafeteria staff, the Financial Aid Department, the deans, the president. Black, Black, Black, Black, Black, Black, Black. The same was true of our neighboring sister schools, Spelman and Clark Atlanta University. Of course, I knew in theory that a historically Black college would consist almost entirely of Black people, but to see it was profound.

The further I drift from those Morehouse days, the more firmly I believe I'll never experience anything else again like them. As I lived them, those days felt ordinary. But they were anything but. Here is one ordinary, extraordinary day:

On this particular morning, like many, I awoke in a bedroom off campus in a brand-new apartment building Morehouse built for upperclassmen, known affectionately as The Suites. My bedroom was just big enough to fit a full-sized bed, a half closet, and a small wooden desk. The bedroom was one of four in an apartment I shared with three Black roommates—my godbrother Jonathan, who I'd known since birth; our friend Justin, who was a junior from Maryland; and a kid named OJ, who was randomly assigned to our room to fill out the apartment. The building was managed by the Morehouse administration. It was located just off campus, close enough to run to class in ten minutes and far enough to feel like you really lived in Atlanta's somewhat dangerous West End neighborhood.

I walked into the common area of our apartment around 8:30 a.m. Between five and ten guys were huddled around a tiny, cheap television watching last night's NBA highlights. Everyone Black. One had thick, square glasses and a Biology textbook on his lap, cramming for a final in thirty minutes. Another wore a tight-fitting wave cap on his head, alternating between tending his waves and scrubbing a pair of Jordans with a toothbrush. A tall sophomore in army fatigues was cooking a grilled cheese sandwich in a frying pan on our stove. He was a member of the Reserve Officer Training Corps program. He clocked my Shaq brand sweatpants as I slid into my flip-flops to head out to class.

"Nigga," he said, a smirk on his face. "Stop wearing those Goddamn Shaq sweatpants. At least wash them, Boulder. Damn!"

The room burst into laughter. I laughed with them. I didn't feel attacked or bullied or othered, the way I would have in a room full of white kids calling me out for my clothes. I felt seen. I felt loved. Camo Guy was actually trying to help me. He knew I didn't have an eye for fashion and was nudging me to take care of myself.

I dapped each guy in the room upon entry. Dapping everyone when entering or exiting a room was a required pleasantry. We joked about the number of high fives you might receive in a day at our college—sometimes upward of one hundred. I'm not kidding. A Black junior from Texas crawled through the window of our apartment to avoid the five-minute walk around through the building's front gate. There was more hysterical laughter. More ribbing. We lived on the first floor and had an open window policy at our place. Anyone was welcome as long as they brought loving vibes and locked the window behind them.

I slipped through the door and headed to Honors English. The classroom was located in a creaky wooden building that looked like it hadn't been renovated since our college was founded in 1867. Our school was born two years after slavery was "abolished," so that Black men could be educated.

Ten Black men and four Black women from Spelman were seated throughout the classroom looking over last night's homework. In the years that followed, one of those students became a top editor at *GQ* and I heard another became the head advisor to Alexandria Ocasio-Cortez. But at the time we were nineteen-year-olds in sweatpants and flip-flops.

Our teacher was a Black thirty-five-year-old woman, a graduate of Howard University and member of AKA Sorority, Incorporated. That day's class focused on detangling Tupac's poetry.

"Okay, y'all, let's look at 'Jada.'" Dr. Lynn handed out photocopies of Tupac's touching ode to his then girlfriend, Jada Pinkett.

"Pay attention to his use of numbers and images instead of words in certain places," she said. "What do you think he meant to imply? For those of you who have taken Shakespeare, what patterns do you recognize between the two of them? How about the way they move between third and first person so sporadically?"

We dissected and compared the writings of those two together, Tupac and Shakespeare. Dr. Lynn wasn't trying to be ironic or provocative by contrasting their styles. She didn't describe Tupac as a *Black* writer in contrast to writers who are white. We were just talking about two prolific writers. That's what made the experience special. I started to understand that I too did not exist only in contrast to whiteness. I just existed.

After class, Dr. Lynn stopped me on the way out. She handed me an essay I'd written, an "A-" scrawled on the corner.

"You know you really have a gift, Chad," she said. It wasn't a compliment. It was a reminder. "There was more meat on the bone than what you wrote here. Why didn't you see it through?"

If I'd had even three teachers like Dr. Lynn in grade school, maybe I would have believed in and honed my writing skills at a younger age. Maybe I would have considered writing as a career sooner. My white teachers in grade school saw that I could write. They gave me A's and asked me to read aloud before the class. But none challenged me to try harder. I had surpassed their low expectations—and that was enough to get by.

After Honors English, I bolted to The Caf for lunch. It was Fried Chicken Wednesday, so the line of people waiting to get inside the cafeteria ran out the door and down the road that divided our campus. When I finally got inside, I swiped my student ID and gave a light church hug to the Black woman smiling at me behind the register. Ms. Gwen lived in the West End. She has been working the Morehouse cafeteria cash register for decades. She's seen thousands of students like me pass through and met every one with a warmth that seemed genuine and set the tone for how we should treat each other once inside.

"I see you still wearing those sweatpants," she said. "Don't let them boys tease you!" Ms. Gwen still remembers me when I stop by campus on trips to Atlanta.

I turned the corner into the wide bowl seating area. Our school's fantastic diversity of Black students was in full bloom. Hundreds of Black students buzzed through The Caf, some seated, some on the table benches, others leaning against walls. Kids from Texas, California, Washington, DC, New York, Wisconsin, Sudan, Egypt, South Africa, Ghana, The Bahamas,

Spain, Australia, Germany, Brazil. Black, Black, Black, Black, Black, Black, Black. Suits, jeans, zip-ups, button-ups, sweatpants, athletic shorts, jerseys, dresses, dreadlocks, waves, high fades, low fades. Black, Black, Black, Black, Black, Black, Black. *Our* music played from the cafeteria speakers. Marvin Gaye, Gucci Mane, Beyoncé, Kanye West, Aretha Franklin, T-Pain. Black, Black, Black, Black, Black.

We didn't hide our faces. We proudly shoveled the delicious chicken, grits, and greens into our mouths after smothering them with hot sauce. We laughed in full-throated, honest bellows. Nobody used the tinny, nasally droning we sometimes forced to seem more palatable in white classrooms and later in corporate offices. No one shrunk himself. We were full there.

The tables were loosely separated into groups: upperclassmen, freshman dorm halls, step teams, band kids, frats, church kids. But there was intermingling and movement back and forth between tables. Everyone was trying to engage with as many other students as possible before the next class. There were some students—Christian Ragin, Brandon Burbage, George Robnett, Marcus Turner—who stayed in The Caf for hours at a time, welcoming droves of students who filed in between classes. They were each tall and sturdy with big smiles, fly dressers and socially adept. They were guardians of The Caf's culture. I don't know if they did it on purpose, but their humor and handshakes offered a refuel for anyone who needed a shot of confidence or joy.

On this particular day, I sat down with the other kids from the DMV—DC, Maryland, and Virginia. Of the fifteen students at the table I knew eight from my hometown in Maryland. Today's discussion was urgent. The 2008 presidential election was a week away and we were stirring about the Democratic nominee, Illinois senator Barack Obama. Black. We were all planning to go and vote for the Black man. That was not a question. But today we were arguing his allegiance to Black people and whether he'd truly represent us.

"Boulder, sit brotha," Burbage commanded. He had a big toothy grin, a bright red North Face jacket, and rare Jordan sneakers I couldn't identify. "Listen to your boy AJ. He's talking crazy."

All fifteen young men leaned into the conversation. A tense argument was afoot and I needed to listen carefully. I might only have a few words to represent my opinion before the argument passed on to the next subject.

AJ, or Ahmad Jahlil, a Political Science major and Sierra Leone immigrant who'd go on to be a DC labor attorney, sat nearby. He was wearing a faded black T-shirt and Chuck Taylor tennis shoes. He was skeptical of Senator Obama.

"What I'm saying isn't crazy at all," Ahmad said. "You're just a casual observer of politics like most Americans so you've totally missed the worst kept secret to the rest of the world. Politicians are bought and puppeted. They're dummies for wealthy people. You guys watch TV shows to get away from real life. You just see a Black man in a suit running for president and think that's gonna do something for you. He's gonna work for the people who pay his campaign bills, like everybody else. This is a cheap trick by white liberals. Put a Black man in office and—"

"Half Black!" Big Martin interrupted.

Eyeballs shifted over to Big Martin from Alabama. He was six-foot-five, 240 pounds, dark-skinned with muscles bulging through his Morehouse Tigers football letterman jacket and a thick Southern accent. He wasn't from the DMV, but nobody would dare tell him to sit elsewhere.

"You think they'd put a Black man up there, with two Black parents, from America, to run for office?" he continued. "You think they'd ever get behind someone who looked like me? This is how they *ease* their way over to a Black president. Start with the light-skinned guy with a white momma."

"Hold up, Martin," Sean from Virginia took the figurative mic. He was biracial. "Having a white mom don't make him any less Black. Y'all are missing the point. You're zooming in too close. This is a really big moment for us. Can you imagine how savvy dude had to be to even get to this point? When he gets in, he's gonna represent us, even if he has to find loopholes to do it. He's just gonna have to do it in the background. He's running for *president*, he's not a civil rights activist."

"And that's exactly the problem," Ahmad said. "Why do we always have to take these baby steps? Boulder, what you think?"

The spotlight was on me. There were many opinions to get to and mine was no more special than the next. That environment taught me to think through my position, state it concisely, and listen closely to the next speaker. I would apply this sort of concise, clear style of communicating later in meetings at Google and in Hollywood network and studio pitches. This was different from my experience in white classrooms, where I spent so much time and energy thinking of ways to mimic the tone and cadence of my classmates so that I could be heard. Then I'd have to choose: bend my point of view to be heard and accepted by classmates and teachers, or speak my bare truth and risk starting another exhausting argument where I'd have to defend my point against an entire classroom. Sometimes by the time I'd actually made my point in those classes I didn't recognize it anymore as my own. In The Caf, I could shoot straight, and I did:

"I mean, I think appearances matter," I said. "Even if Barack doesn't do anything in policy to advance Black people, just seeing someone like us in that office is meaningful. I already feel different just knowing that he's running. Imagine the impact on kids who are four years old right now. Their first memory will be living in a country led by a Black man."

The conversation went on another twenty minutes, until guys peeled off to empty their trays and head to their next classes. We never reached any sort of consensus on the matter, but we all had our chance to be heard and we each learned from the others. That was more important than consensus because we each left with a wide array of perspectives to consider as we individually decided how to cast our votes. And we all had a chance to be heard.

After class, there was always a party. Seven days a week for four years, I knew I could go out around 10 p.m. and have an amazing night. House parties, nightclubs, Atlanta bars and restaurants were all packed with beautiful young Black people and blaring the latest hip-hop and R&B or classic funk, soul, disco, or Motown. Our shit. Atlanta was the center of Black music, which was becoming the center of pop music. In the late aughts, hip-hop and trap music took prominence in the mainstream with Atlanta acts including Outkast, Young Jeezy, Gucci Mane, T.I., and Southern superstars like Lil Wayne and T-Pain leading the way. Our school was right in the middle of it all and you could feel the tremblings from thudding car speakers at any time of day or night.

The party that trumped all others came a few days later, on November 4, 2008. Hundreds of Black college students, myself included, crowded into Spelman College's Lower Manley Student Center. We watched CNN on TVs mounted from the high ceilings of the bottom level of the student center. The din of the crowd was much louder than the volume on the TVs, so we were left to read Obama and Senator John McCain's facial expressions and decode the confusing electoral college maps to determine who was winning the election. During commercials, DJ Bruckup piped in loud music. We danced to break from the tension. "2 Step" by T-Pain. "Walk It Out" by Unk. "Lollipop" by Lil Wayne.

"I can't believe this," Anita said. "I honestly never thought we would have a Black president. Not in my lifetime. Not ever." Each freshman at Morehouse and Spelman was assigned a partner at the other school during freshman orientation, to foster strong ties between the institutions. Anita was my assigned partner who had become a real friend.

"Shh," I said. "Don't jinx it." She chuckled.

"You're always so paranoid. He's gonna win. Look at him."

I looked at Senator Obama on the screen. Poised. Handsome. Solid.

Wow.

He was gonna win. She was right. I am not easily swept away by the emotion in politics or elections, but this felt different. This felt like history. Sure enough, moments later, President Obama was announced as the winner of the 2008 presidential election.

The room erupted in cheers. I hugged Anita. We danced, and yelled, and roared, and laughed. There was nowhere on earth I wanted to be more in that moment than right where I was: at Spelman College, celebrating with my people.

We spilled out onto Westview Drive, the road that connects Morehouse, Spelman, and Clark. Thankfully, Young Jeezy had been thoughtful enough to provide us with a soundtrack for this moment. His hit single, "My President Is Black" (featuring Nas) blasted from car speakers all around us, while the cars themselves idled donuts through the crowds of jubilant Black teenagers and young adults.

> *My President is Black, My Lambo's blue,*
> *And I be God damn if my rims ain't too.*

My friend Earl, the barrel-chested star linebacker on the football team, was driving his Range Rover in circles blasting the Young Jeezy anthem. He smashed his car horn over and over. I jumped into the SUV and stood on the passenger seat hanging out the open door looking out over the crowds. As far as I could see in every direction, young Black people were dancing, hugging, jumping, shouting, calling parents and friends, holding their cell phones up to take in the noise. There were sparklers sizzling and fireworks blasting off. People popped champagne bottles right there in the street all over campus.

I was overcome by it all. I took full, deep breaths.

I never again felt such a deep connection to so many Black people at once. I've never since seen so many Black folks smiling and crying unembarrassed tears of joy in the same place. Not at a wedding, not at a graduation, or a Baptism, or a concert or a family reunion. The pride and weightless happiness I felt in the sea of Black people around me that night will always be at the core of Barack Obama's legacy for me.

I think we all knew there would be a time to debate and analyze President Obama's politics as we had in the cafeteria. We'd have our moment to arbitrate whether or not he was doing his part to represent us. But that night, we had to act up until morning and nobody could stop us. Because the President was Black. And we were too. And that was plenty reason for a party.

GRAYSON BROWN

"I thought that I, as a human, could transcend racial dynamics. That is really dangerous, because eventually something happens that snaps you back and white people show you very clearly, and often quite damagingly to your person, that you're not the same."

Grayson is the chief financial officer at a tech startup valued at $250 million according to the *Wall Street Journal*. He recently led a $100 million fundraising series for the company. Previously, Grayson led tech, media, and telecom investments as a senior investment analyst at Klay Advisors LLC, a hedge fund. His professional journey spans Wall Street, including stops as director of strategy and business development at a large venture capital fund and analyst work at a well-known investment bank.

I first met Grayson in college. He landed at Morehouse after he left an elite, mostly white liberal arts college in New England, an event we discuss in our conversation below. After Morehouse, Grayson ascended the Wall Street ranks as fast as any Black man I know, before eventually making his transition to the tech world. I wanted to talk to him about what he learned from his jarring transition from racial isolation at his previous university to the sea of Blackness at Morehouse. Our interview took place in Grayson's Fort Greene apartment with high ceilings, spacious by New York standards. We sat on a long, beige couch with a giant, framed photo of the moon hanging on the off-white wall behind us. Grayson told me the story of being called a "nigger" by one of his frat brothers in an otherwise all-white fraternity at the university. Grayson defended himself and was expelled from school shortly thereafter. Grayson surprisingly thinks the incident saved his life because the resulting tailspin landed him at Morehouse, where he began to understand and embrace his identity.

I admired Grayson's bravery as he shared that dark moment. I could tell by his flat, detached tone he's replayed everything that led him to that fight. He's dissected everything that happened in the fallout too. It must be scary and embarrassing to admit that Grayson let himself believe he was safe in what seemed to him to be such a totally white environment. He says he won't let himself completely trust whiteness again in a way that exposes him to the same humiliation and helplessness. I wonder, won't that limit his opportunities for deep friendships with white people and professional growth? Grayson accepts that it will. That is a trade-off he's willing to make. But he learned through it all—the slur, the fight, the tailspin, and his eventual landing in the restorative comfort of an HBCU—that he was never alone, but only separated from his community, and he had the backbone to defend himself even when he felt alone.

Chad: What does the term "racial duality" evoke for you?

Grayson: Much of my background and family is rooted in a strong Black culture, but the reality is that we live in a very white-dominated world. To function, Black people must, at a minimum, present things in a way that can be consumed and understood by people who don't share the same sort of cultural background as us. So, I personally would rather not think in terms of duality—meaning two different people—but two different ways of communicating and interacting. This is probably not just for Black people, but for people who come from minority groups in any way, as a necessity to be a productive person in a white world.

Chad: Is there anything about racial duality that *is* unique to a Black experience?

Grayson: Our people's history is unique. You're a Black person living in a white world. The history of Black people in this white world, particularly in the United States, is such that you naturally need to be somewhat skeptical of certain parts of that world. It's tough to describe. I grew up in all-white schools. My approach to operating in that all-white world was to push away some of my Black culture and try to really assimilate. I tried to assimilate to the point where I wasn't just trying to present things in ways that were acceptable to white people, but more so I tried to change myself and my background. I tried to delude myself into believing that white people and I were the same and we could meet on the same level. I tried to believe that it wasn't about learning how to operate in their world, because it was my world too. Because we were the same. I adopted all their mannerisms. I tried to dress like them, talk like them, force myself to have very similar views on the world.

I went to college. I became the first Black president of a white fraternity. I was later kicked out over a racially charged fight, though I'd rather not say exactly how. The fraternity, guys who had elected me president, wrote a letter to the school saying I was a dangerous threat to them. Anyone who knows me knows I wasn't and have never been a particularly violent guy. It has taken many years to appreciate exactly what occurred there, but as I've interpreted it through the years, it showed me how dangerous it is for a Black person to pretend to be white.

Now, after Trump's election, which was so obviously racially and culturally divisive, more of us are forced to accept the same reality that I was forced to accept. Race matters.

Chad: In what particular ways?

Grayson: There are stark differences in experiences between races; differences in the ways that we interpret various situations. The support of your affinity group matters. That is inescapable. I was guilty of convincing myself that I was so charming or so great that I could transcend my person. I thought that I, as a human, could transcend racial dynamics. That is really dangerous, because eventually something happens that snaps you back and white people show you very clearly, and often quite damagingly to your person, that you're not the same. You're reminded, then, that there are differences, and that there are biases. That was my experience at the university. So when you talk about duality—you know—it's something that has evolved in me over time. But only for a very short period of my life have I lived a truly dual lifestyle.

Chad: What you're saying is that you were not living in duality at all. You forced yourself to take the pill of whiteness so thoroughly that you believed you had taught yourself to live with one identity, which mirrored the white people around you.

Grayson: Yep.

Chad: Describe your upbringing.

Grayson: I grew up in the Washington, DC, area for most of my life. When I was a young child, we moved to Prince George's County, Maryland, which is a majority Black county. My mother is a psychologist. My dad is a mechanic. My dad is from Trinidad. My mom has advanced degrees. My dad stopped at high school but he's a pretty competent guy. My mom and my uncle, who were very core to me growing up, had an air of seeming like they came from more money than they actually came from. My mom grew up reading books. My great-grandmother had a room full of books in her house. There were some things about my background that would probably lead one to believe that we were fancier than we actually were.

Chad: At what age did you start taking classes primarily with white kids?

Grayson: Middle school.

Chad: Is that where you learned the value of adapting fully to white sensibilities?

Grayson: Yeah. I went to an expensive, private all-boys school in Maryland. The headmaster decided that year to make a big diversity push. [In my opinion], he was not very smart about the execution. He basically admitted everyone [Black] who applied. So, he brought a bunch of Black kids in that year. I graduated with one or two Black kids in my class my senior year [after all the attrition]. But through the course of my time at private school, from middle school through high school, there were twelve Black kids. All the other Black kids got kicked out or left for various reasons. Many of the kids at private school—Black and white—were, candidly, bullshitters.

When I got there, I wasn't one. I was studying. Every day of my childhood, I'd sit at the dining room table and do my homework for five hours every night and then go to sleep. I'd wake up. I'd go to school and I'd start all over again. Every fucking day.

My mom is bookish. I have vivid memories of spending all day with my mom at Howard University library. We would spend all day in bookstores. All fucking day. Just reading. She would do her work and I would play with books. That was my life. So when I got to private school, the course work stepped up and I had tons of work to do.

My mom will never forget one story. We took one kid from my class to go visit my grandparents in Delaware with us. We did what we always did on the weekends: we went to the library and sat in there all day studying, doing work. That kid went back to school and made a big deal of it, telling all the kids they wouldn't believe what Grayson does on the weekends; how hard he works and how hard he studies.

That was very much a turning point for me because it showed that I was fundamentally different from many of the Black kids in the class. In a way that was most superficially identifiable to me—a teenager—I felt more like the white kids than the Black kids. That was when I thought I had to make a choice. I needed to fit in with the people with whom I thought I had more in common: white people. I needed to see the world and act and be like them. That turning point was seventh grade. From then on, I was progressively consuming whiteness more and more.

The reality is if you go to school two hours away and spend four hours each night doing homework, there wasn't enough time spent present with my family for them to offset the cultural training I got in the private school environment. The vast majority of my time was spent with those white folks. And the few Black people I really knew outside my family weren't doing much. I didn't feel connected to them.

Jack and Jill didn't let me in. They didn't think my mom was good enough. As much as I should hold some grudge against them, that organization is considerably valuable. I needed it because I did not know enough Black people. I did not know there was diversity among Black people but there were still things that tied us together.

Chad: So, while at private school, you found your connection to the other white students felt stronger than your connection to the other Black students . . .

Grayson: The Black kids also shunned me . . .

Chad: Because of your perceived connection to the white kids?

Grayson: Well, there was no connection. It was just that I was corny and the white kids were cool. The white people often looked to the cool Black people to determine who was cool among the Black people. So when the Black kids dismissed me, I had to try extra hard to get the white people to include me. Because otherwise I would have just been alone.

Chad: Once you recognized that was the equation, what did you do? What did you steer into? What did you amplify about yourself to endear yourself to the white kids?

Grayson: I stopped studying as much. My private school was a highly athletic school. I started taking sports very seriously. I changed the way I dressed. Even more ridiculous shit. Do you know who Armstrong Williams is?

Chad: No.

Grayson: I would describe Armstrong Williams as a Black, conservative radio host in the vein of Rush Limbaugh. He's also a Trump advisor. This was early 2000s in DC, at a conservative, white, all-boys school, with George W. Bush as president. I was operating within a highly conservative environment. I convinced myself that I was a Black Republican. I did an internship at Armstrong Williams's office. I was really trying. I have vivid memories of getting into serious arguments with my mom and stepfather when I would take up for white people for systemic and outright race crimes.

Chad: As a kid?

Grayson: As a fucking kid. I was really digging my heels in on whiteness. I warped myself. Maybe it doesn't have to be that extreme for everyone, but I think it was very dangerous for me.

Chad: What did you perceive as the cost if you didn't bring yourself that way? If you didn't adopt that theology? Was the cost alienation? Was it inertia? Did you feel like you weren't really presented with options?

Grayson: I had a pretty good lifestyle coming up. I was far from poor. But the first time I went to some kid's house whose Dad was the CEO of a big public company it changed my perspective. I thought it was incredible. I needed to endear myself to those people. I wanted to live like them. I wanted those people to feel comfortable with me. I wanted to be in their world.

That is probably a more mature outlook. At the time, I was just a middle school kid. I wanted to be liked. I wanted to be cool. I wanted the girls from [sister school] Holton-Arms to want to dance with me at the middle school dance. And there were just way more white kids than me.

Before I went to private school, I was class president of my Black elementary school and school president. I was valedictorian. I was captain of my little league football team. But when I got to private school, none of that mattered. I wanted to be popular and cool. I realized that to have those things I needed to give something up to do it. I needed to become more like them.

It was subconscious. My uncle used to buy me Jordans, but then one day I asked for Sperrys. I gave up jeans for khakis. I wasn't at home enough. I didn't have kids that were away from that world enough to tell me what I was giving up was more than shoes and pants.

Chad: Is there anything you did growing up through those experiences that became second nature? Do you wield any of those adaptations as power today?

Grayson: Trivial behaviors. Oftentimes, when big powerful companies, banks, and firms hire high-performing Black kids, those students struggle with soft skills upon entry. They don't know how to talk to white people. They don't know how to interact. The companies don't know how to manage young Black people. They don't know how not to offend them. They just don't get it.

The unique people can go from Black settings and then quickly pick up how to operate in those other worlds. For me it was the complete opposite. I knew how to operate with white people. That has not been a challenge for me in a very, very long time. I can wield that. But it's subconscious. When I show up to meet with a bank and the other guy shows up wearing a Patagonia vest, under a Patagonia coat, I recognize him. I know his mannerisms.

Chad: Does it bring out a different part of you? Do you then evoke a certain tone, a certain posture, a certain way of eye contact? Are all those things happening subconsciously or are you actually spending brain power on them?

Grayson: I don't change who I am. Now, I consciously make an effort not to change who I am. I am very serious about being 99 percent the same guy. There are topics that I might bring up with a double Patagonia guy that I might not bring up with a dude from Howard. But if those topics come up, I am not changing my view on them. I am not expressing something different than what I fundamentally believe. The reason for that is what happened at the university followed by my experience at Morehouse.

At Morehouse I realized there are so many Black men in this world and I can be Black, fully Black, and be different. And be similar to that guy with the double Patagonia. And it does not compromise my Blackness at all.

I make a conscious decision every day that I am not going to change who I am. I might say "nigga" a little more often around Black people, but I'm not changing what I say to people under any circumstances. It's just not worth it. Going to Morehouse was the beginning of a multiyear process of finally coming to terms with who I am aside from Blackness; aside from trying to be white; aside from finance. Who the fuck is

Grayson? I have gotten to a place where I'm semi-comfortable with who that is, so I'm not gonna compromise him.

Chad: When was the turning point moment?

Grayson: My sophomore year of college.

Chad: You show up to the university as a freshman on the football team. What perspective did you get on fraternity life? What did it represent for you? Why were you interested?

Grayson: I wanted to be cool. The fraternity had a big house. They threw parties. It was a football fraternity. The majority of the kids in my freshman class on the football team pledged the fraternity. It seemed like fun so I jumped in.

Chad: How did you become president of the fraternity?

Grayson: I wanted to be a leader. I wanted to be respected and liked. To me, that meant becoming the president. It was a shit-show fraternity. The job was herding a bunch of drunk, big athlete dudes all the time and trying to organize. After a year in the fraternity I knew what the place needed to do to run. I was the only semi-sober, responsible dude around there, so congratulations.

That's partially what made it all really frustrating. I was holding the fraternity up. The university is a liberal school, but the fraternities were largely populated by athletes. People go to the university because they want to go to a liberal place and be free and radical thinkers. The athletes go to the university because it's a really good school and they got in. They don't go there because they're seeking an alternative lifestyle. So, there is a friction between athletes and the broader community that is more pronounced than at other schools. The friction is so pronounced that the school has discussed removing fraternities altogether for the last twenty years. But every year, some rich donor who graduated in the fucking 1950s who loves his fraternity sends the president of his fraternity to go speak on behalf of the fraternity. I even joined the university's student government at one point to represent on the fraternity's behalf. I collected the rent for the house. I would clean up after parties I organized.

I'd present a friendly face of the fraternity and be the mature person. I saved these motherfuckers constantly. So when they as a group decided to fuck me, it couldn't have possibly been a more clear statement. The guy who I hit was unilaterally known to be a complete fucking asshole. He was almost flunking out of school; a dirtbag to every girl around; drunk, arrogant, douchebag. People thought he was cool but he was a complete prick.

[Below, Grayson refers to an incident where he and the aforementioned fraternity brother got into a heated argument. His fraternity brother called him a "nigger." Grayson responded physically.]

I could not have possibly imagined that they would write a letter saying that I was dangerous because they were afraid that I was going to tell the school that he called me a nigger. That was their way. They did it before the trial. That was their way of preventing their own liability. They told campus officials that what they needed to know is that they considered me a threat.

This is the part I didn't really want to mention because it's embarrassing. I normally don't mention that he called me a nigger. The reason I don't do that is because I did not mention that to the board during the trial because I'm a pretty loyal person. I did not want to ruin him. All the while I knew that he was destroying me. I could not bring myself to do it.

Chad: You called it a turning point. Was there a moment where you realized this was something big? Was it after you were expelled? Once you arrived at Morehouse?

Grayson: It was the first time that my parents pointed out that these white guys were conspiring against me and I had no alternative argument. In the past I always tried to rationalize seemingly ugly actions by white people. In this moment I just couldn't explain it away. I realized these were not my people. They do not have my best interests at heart and I need to be cautious around them. I can't fully trust these folks.

Chad: And where does that conflict sit in your brain now? Specifically, I mean the understanding that no matter what, a race line is a line. Where does that sit in your brain now?

Grayson: I had a very big event that occurred in my life that taught me a lesson. If I expose myself to that same thing that bit me in the ass again, I will regret it enormously. It's not like I don't have white friends, but I am only willing to expose myself to people who I believe have a bias, beyond my charm, to not harm me. Because if they did harm me and I knew that there was this thing that lingered in them that could possibly harm me and they harmed me, I would have a very hard time not regretting that. So with white people I know there is nothing really core to them that will make them not harm me. And that leads me to be less inclined to expose myself to them and really trust them as a group.

Chad: Is that distrust active? Is it conscious? Does it take up space? Does it come at a cost?

Grayson: Unless I live in a world where all white people cannot be trusted, then yes it comes at a cost. The trust line with them is much shorter so I'm not as willing to really dive into things fully with them. I probably have missed and will continue to miss great opportunities because of that distrust. At the same time, I will not look up and be fucked the same way I was fucked previously.

My mother went to pick up my transcripts after I was expelled because I was banned from campus. When my mom went to go pick up my transcripts, the registrar said to my mom, "Should your son decide that he wants to continue his studies somewhere else . . ."

My mom was outraged. She thought, *Of course he's going to finish school. This is not going to end him. This is not going to be the thing that destroys him.* Getting kicked out of school for a violent action is something that could really destroy someone's life. I don't believe that we have an infinite number of things like that that we can overcome in our lives. So I would have a very hard time forgiving myself for exposing myself to the same type of risk again.

Yes, distrust comes at cost, and honestly my measurement of that cost is subconscious at this point. If a white person asks me a question to which my answer could potentially make that person uncomfortable, I will not change my answer. But I probably will avoid engaging in that conversation. I will deflect it as much as I possibly can. If I'm backed in the corner, I'm going to tell that person my answer.

Chad: How have you applied lessons from your Black experience in your work?

Grayson: One of the things that struck me most upon arriving at Morehouse was the all-pervasive side hustle. Given weird, less-than-perfect financial backgrounds growing up, nearly all of my classmates found unique ways to make money on the side during their studies at Morehouse. I think this is something I've held close to my heart. I've advised at least ten start-ups with creative ideas over the years. Some hits, mostly flops, but they've allowed me to express.

I'm not particularly innovative, but I've been able to add value in investing circles because I have a *different* view than those who are normally capital allocators. I understand an entirely different swath of people on a more intimate level than my white peers, which allows me to take a different approach on investments and gives me somewhat of an edge.

In 2010, the median wealth, or net worth, for Black families was $4,900, compared to median wealth for whites of $97,000. This is always in the back of my mind. I want to save the world. I want to change the lives of each individual kid I encounter. But, I believe the single best thing I can do for my community, and for the country, is make money and give my kids my morals and worldview and the platform, freedom, and resources necessary to actualize that worldview. Yes, I make charitable donations. Yes, I mentor constantly. Yes, I engage in all kinds of different ways with people in my community to try and make a difference. However, what we need is a class of Black people who have real values and can empathize with the broader community and who have the resources and space and freedom they need to affect real sustained change. That's where I think I need to play.

LATEESHA THOMAS

"I never assumed I would be able to just climb a normal corporate ladder and get the things I want. So, I've always had to take a step back to figure out how things are working. What are the complex interconnected relationships between both people and teams? How can I play that to my benefit to get the things I want within an organization?"

LaTeesha is the CEO and cofounder of Onramp, an Oakland-based tech startup that aims to solve the technical workforce hiring crisis by helping tech giants like Google and Pandora train and hire technical talent from diverse backgrounds. LaTeesha is also a technologist, conference organizer, speaker, and advocate for diversity and inclusion in tech. Formerly she managed partnerships for Google's Women Techmakers initiative. Before that she was director of business development at Dev Bootcamp, which was sold to Kaplan during her time there. I met LaTeesha at Dev Bootcamp. She was a colleague who became a true friend.

LaTeesha is one of very few Black women to have raised venture capital millions to run her tech startup. Less than 15 percent of venture capital funding in the US goes to women, and less than 1 percent goes to African-American and Latinx founders. LaTeesha has beaten the odds, all the while being labeled "aggressive" and "unpleasant" by micro-aggressing colleagues. In that way, her journey reminded me of Jewel's, but Lateesha's magic is all her own: in our conversation, she pointed to her ability to learn and master systems as the characteristic that allows her to beat the odds as an entrepreneur. And she learned how to master systems at a small, predominantly white college where she had to design her own experience to thrive.

I admire LaTeesha's unsparing point of view on her industry. She explained that at some point her approach to dealing with a tech industry largely run by white and Asian men hardened. She won't wait for them to change anymore, she says. She'll work the system to take what's theirs.

Chad: How did you grow up, LaTeesha?

LaTeesha: Well, I grew up in Monterey, California. Monterey is predominantly white and the city right next to it, Seaside, is predominantly Black. The vast majority of my family lived in Seaside. I lived in Monterey with my mom starting in middle school. So in middle school and high school I went to majority white schools with people whose families made way more money than mine.

Chad: How was your educational experience?

LaTeesha: I went to a tiny liberal arts school in the middle of New England. Even though I went to a predominantly white high school, I never felt the real shock of being around white people 100 percent of the time because of my family. My school was a really tiny campus called Bard College at Simon's Rock. There were only about 250 freshmen. Of the 250 freshmen, there were about 10 Black students on campus. I knew every single one of them and every single one of them knew me. We were all very different and weren't necessarily friends, but it was just sort of acknowledged that we knew of each other's presence and we understood each other's experiences.

That was the first time I started to think about structural racism and structural inequality as a concept that was real to me. I mean, I heard things from my mom growing up, like, "You've gotta be five times better or ten times better, work ten times harder." And so I understood that race played a role in my life, but it was the first time that I had a real, visceral reaction to the inequality. And that was primarily as a result of coming from a single-parent family. We didn't have a lot of money so most of the time I couldn't really pay to be in school. So every single semester we were just constantly behind on paying tuition. So I'd do these gymnastics with the administration to be able to register for classes on time.

As a result, I started to get more into thinking about how systems of inequalities work and ways in which I could defend myself in that system to make change. And not just that, but I also thought about how to figure out how to game the system by understanding it. I thought about how to game the system in order to create a better experience for myself. Here's a silly example. At Bard College you could create themed housing if you wanted to try to secure better housing for yourself. You could create a theme house and have people apply to live in it. So most students might create a house specifically focused on engineering for people interested in computer programming. So we created a Black house. It was just me and my three friends who wanted to live together. We tried to call it a Black Student

Union and applied for it. What were they going to tell us? No? But we really just wanted better housing for the four of us as sophomores. We applied for it and the administration was like, "We legit cannot tell these four Black women that they can't have their fake Black Student Union–themed housing."

So sometimes it was as silly as that. Or sometimes it was more serious. I was on a committee that worked with the deans of all the major educational programs within the school—like the heads of the science, language, and literature departments. I was elected to this committee that would approve all of the new course work and decide which courses would be taught every semester. I was able to get the school to create "Diversity Day," which was a name I hated. But it was essentially a day where the entire school shut down classes to instead just talk about issues of race and inequality. There were different workshops and non-structured conversations throughout the day. It was actually a pretty expensive endeavor for a school to cancel classes for a day.

Chad: So how have you applied your understanding of working through frameworks as an adult? How has that stayed with you through your professional career?

LaTeesha: I think I have just always had an understanding that I was never gonna go through the front door for anything, and so . . .

Chad: Because of your race?

LaTeesha: Uh, yeah, I would say that. Because of a mix of my race and my gender.

Chad: Mmhmm.

LaTeesha: Let's take Dev Bootcamp for example. Dev Bootcamp was an immersive coding school that you and I both worked for. They had this really interesting system of management called Holacracy which was essentially a gamified way of governing groups of people in a seemingly flat, but not actually flat, company. You had to be able to understand all these rules in order to really participate in a meaningful way in the structure of the organization.

A lot of people within that organization felt really disenfranchised because they didn't understand the rules and didn't understand how to navigate within those rules and felt like they didn't have a voice in what was happening within the organization. A good amount of those people who felt disenfranchised were white. And I just found it to be really funny because they don't understand how, in the world, the system works in their favor all the time. This was the one time where they had to figure out how to navigate within this little bitty world that had been created and had been constructed. And they couldn't do it. And they just refused to do it, because they were used to being able to operate within the systems that work for them.

But "The System" had never worked for me in any context. So when I encountered this new managerial system, instead of expecting for it to work for me, I studied and learned how to use it, and I think that was the primary reason why I was able to accumulate influence and authority within that organization. I came in as an operations manager, which was basically an officer manager role. I came in at what was one of the lowest level roles in the company and ended up as the head of partnerships and business development. In that time, I saw many people who had come in with a lot of authority leave very quickly or fall off along the way because they just couldn't figure out how to work within that system.

I just never had that assumption that things were going to be given to me. I never assumed I would be able to just climb a normal corporate ladder and get the things I want. So, I've always had to take a step back to figure out how things are working. What are the complex interconnected relationships between both people and teams? How can I play that to my benefit to get the things I want within an organization?

Chad: You are a businessperson and a technologist. You know the premise of the book states that there are things we learn from enduring and experiencing Blackness in this country that can be applied to advance ourselves in business, science, art, etc. Do you believe that's true? Why or why not?

LaTeesha: Yes I do. And I also feel it's hard to quantify. It's hard to describe. Business, or whatever you're doing, is about relationships. It's about people and how people work together and influence and power. As a Black person you have to be hyperaware in every moment of how you're being perceived by the people around you. You have to be hyperaware of how you're showing up in the world. And not just when you go to work, but when you're walking down the street and having conversations with people. In order to protect yourself, to stay alive, you have to be hyperaware of how your presence is affecting other people. And not because you've done anything wrong, but because history has shown that people's perceptions of you may not necessarily match the way that you see yourself or the way people who know you experience you. But sometimes those perceptions can be really powerful and sometimes those perceptions can override somebody's logical thinking and cause them to have an emotion that could ultimately be harmful to you.

In being hyperaware of how you're showing up, you develop a level of empathy that is so necessary, no matter what industry you're in. And being able to read people and to read situations around you makes you a better leader.

In being hyperaware of how you're showing up, I think that level of empathy is so necessary, no matter what industry you're in. And that level of empathy makes you better at reading situations and people than most. That can help you figure out how to plug in and be helpful and be useful.

Chad: I've had a really close seat to watch your ascendance in the tech industry over the last, I guess . . . five years? Where do you think your drive comes from?

La Teesha: If you had asked me this five years ago, I would have said I want to help create an industry that is more equitable and inclusive for people who look like me. And not just people who look like me, but people who don't look like the dominant demographic in the industry. Now, instead of trying to get the industry to change, I'm far more interested in carving out spaces of my own and helping support people to carve out spaces of their own. The only way we'll see a significant shift in the industry is by having our own large, billion-dollar unicorn companies that are Black-owned or women-run or Latinx-run. Until we start to carve out market share and compete seriously with the big companies run by white and Asian men, we're not going to really see any significant shifts within the industry. It's a little naive to think that we would. It's naive to think, specifically in tech, that there would be a shift in the dynamics within an industry run by white and Asian dudes. It just seems illogical to me. And instead of getting them to change, I'm more interested in just taking what is theirs.

Chad: How would you advise a young Black person to find success in the tech startup world without sacrificing her cultural identity? Is there a way she could use that identity as a source of strength?

LaTeesha: Yeah, I don't know. This may not be the best advice, but I am becoming better at compartmentalizing my life. I just have to realize that I'm not going to get everything I need from my work life. In order to supplement, I have to build a community around me of like-minded folks in my industry to reaffirm my experience so that when something happens to me at work, and I don't really feel like I can speak out on it in the moment, I can go back and talk to somebody who's had a similar experience. I have to be able to talk to someone who can say, "Yes, that happened. No, you're not crazy. They're probably gaslighting you, but you're not crazy. I hear you and I see you." That's been really important to me.

Your words have power but so does your silence. I've observed this in one of my close friends recently. She doesn't give people any more of her revenge than she feels they deserve. Whether that means in a moment somebody has said something wild or offensive or hurtful in a meeting, they don't deserve to see her pain. They don't deserve to see her anger. They don't deserve to see any part of her, and so she just doesn't give it to them. And it's so impressive to me. That's not how I used to be. I used to wear my emotions on my sleeve. Even if I wasn't saying anything, you could see on my face how I felt about a situation. Her poker face is like no one else's. And I'll think that she has nothing to say and then we'll get into a separate space and she'll unload and tell me everything that she's thinking and feeling. She just doesn't feel that the person deserves any part of her. So she just doesn't give them anything.

So, I would say, figure out what it is you want to share with people and how open you want to be, and if they don't deserve it and they haven't earned it, then don't give it to them. That can be really difficult. It makes you feel like sometimes you're choking down what you're feeling or what you're experiencing. But that doesn't mean you have to never let it out. It just means that you don't have to let it out then. You're not going to change their behavior and it's not going to make a difference to them. But getting your experience reaffirmed by somebody else who has experienced it before can make all the difference.

DR. CAROL ESPY-WILSON

"My husband began his career at MIT by conducting an interview-based research study of the experiences of Black students. One student spoke for many when he said MIT is a good place to be from but not a good place to be at."

Dr. Espy-Wilson is an electrical engineer and professor in the Electrical and Computer Engineering Department and the Institute for Systems Research at the University of Maryland. She earned a BS in Electrical Engineering from Stanford University, and an MS, EE, and PhD in Electrical Engineering from the Massachusetts Institute of Technology. Dr. Espy-Wilson's more recent research analyzes speech as a behavioral signal for emotion recognition, sentiment analysis, and the detection and monitoring of mental health. She is also the founder of OmniSpeech, a software technology company that aims to revolutionize the enhancement of voice communication in speech-enabled applications and in digital mobile devices. Prior to joining the faculty at the University of Maryland, Dr. Espy-Wilson was a faculty member at Boston University.

Dr. Espy-Wilson is married to Dr. John Wilson, once the president of Morehouse College. But I've known Dr. Espy-Wilson for most of my life as a close friend to my godmother, who was also raised in Georgia. People like Dr. Espy-Wilson—Black scientists—are hidden heroes. Media coverage tends to track Black entertainers, politicians, and athletes, so our doctors and scientists often go unnoticed. I think this makes it harder for young Black people to visualize themselves as doctors and scientists, even if those are the professions that their talents best serve. I wanted to talk to someone who not only served as an example to Black kids who aspire to work in science, but who saw her own professional dreams through in a field so dominated by whiteness.

Throughout her career, Dr. Espy-Wilson experienced overt racism and sexism. In our interview, she described microaggressions she faced during her post-secondary education—a professor avoiding her in the hallways, a male fellow student repeatedly asking her out without any real interest, just to make her feel small and powerless. One professor even went so far as to tell her to transfer to another school because she didn't "belong."

Dr. Espy-Wilson described her grad school as an obstacle to overcome, rather than opportunity. But she did overcome it. Her faith in God born in her upbringing in Atlanta Baptist churches gave her fuel. She was also pushed by the knowledge that her own father, a smart and talented man, never had the chance to face such an obstacle. His chance at higher education was limited because of his race. Dr. Espy-Wilson was determined to be different, even if she had to withstand bullying at each stop. Her Black Magic is perseverance and bravery.

———

Chad: How did you grow up, Dr. Wilson?

Carol: I grew up in Atlanta, Georgia, in an all-Black community. I started out in Decatur, Georgia, in the projects, and then I think around second grade, we moved to Kirkwood. That was in Atlanta. We bought a home. I would say a low-income neighborhood, but I never would have known that we weren't middle class. We were not middle class, but I never wanted or needed for anything. I had three older brothers—one fourteen years older, one thirteen years older, one seven years older. So my two older brothers were sort of father figures for me as well because my mom and dad separated when I was three. They all had very high expectations of me.

My brothers went to college and it was just assumed I would go to college. It was never a question. They were all very good in math and I assumed I would just be good in math.

They lived at home and so I got a chance to see them doing

all their work. They set a really good example for me, and encouraged me, particularly the one who was seven years older because we were closer in age and in the house together a lot more. He was always trying to teach me the material he was learning. He was an electrical engineer and went to Georgia Tech. Both of my oldest two brothers went to Morehouse College in Atlanta. The second oldest wanted to be an engineer, so he ended up being the second Black to graduate from Georgia Tech. He went off and became a navy pilot.

Chad: So you started off in the projects, you moved to another all-Black community that was, um, lower-middle-class as you described it—

Carol: I wouldn't say middle-class at all.

Chad: Lower-class.

Carol: Lower-class.

Chad: What was it that made you and your brothers so ambitious? What was it that made you such high achievers? Why do you think that happened?

Carol: My mother had two brothers that lived on the other side of town. They lived in a middle-class neighborhood. My uncle and my mother were very close, and I know that my uncle helped to put my two older brothers through college. And we had cousins. Those brothers had cousins that were around their age as well, and those cousins also went to college. So I think it was probably the extended family.

Chad: Mmm.

Carol: And my father was really smart and very ambitious. He was great at math, even though he never finished high school. He had stopped high school to help his mother because their father left, so he had to go to work. But he was really good at putting in kitchens and bathrooms and things like that. They said he could come into a room and do a lot of math just in his head and know the materials and how to lay it out. So my two older brothers had to work with my dad before he became an alcoholic.

I was three and my two older brothers were sixteen and seventeen when my dad left. So they had him most of the time that they were growing up, and there was a long period of time when my father was not an alcoholic. In fact, my brothers said he became an alcoholic because he was really smart and ambitious but he was Black so he was not able to accomplish the things that he really wanted to accomplish. He got passed over and had a lot of disappointments in his life. But I don't know all the story because I was too young. You don't think to ask a lot of questions about that when you're young. But what I've come to understand is that my father was crushed because he wasn't able to achieve what he knew he could achieve if he had the opportunity.

So, I think my dad also set a really good example for my older brothers. And my younger brother got to see some of that as well. I missed all of that because most of my memories of my dad are of visiting him, but while he was sick. He would see things in the room that weren't there. I'd visit him in the hospital. So, I didn't get to see him when he wasn't suffering from that disease.

Chad: And after you came up in Atlanta, you went to Stanford for college. Was there a culture shock for you when you got to Stanford?

Carol: Yes, definitely. I visited Stanford when I was in high school because my mom and I went out to visit my brother, who had just completed his masters degree in Electrical Engineering. So I had seen the campus, but I was young and I really wasn't paying attention to it. When I went there, it was very different because I was the only Black in many of my classes. I was the only African-American majoring in Electrical Engineering my year at Stanford so that was something that took getting used to. I was in classrooms with people who were socially awkward.

Chad: Mmhmm.

Carol: Many engineers are that way. And I'm not socially awkward at all. I'd been quite popular in high school. There was a guy, Armando, who was Chicano. I don't know what his environment was in terms of the diversity where he went to high school, but he came up to me after seeing the grade I got on an exam and said, "Hey, would you like to study together?" And he and I studied together for the rest of our time there. But then others joined our group because we were doing really well. So other white guys asked to join our group, and I remember this one guy who saw me as a sexual object. He could never not comment on my physical appearance. "Oh, we ought to go out for a drink." or "We oughta hang out," you know. It was just constant and I would talk to Armando a few times to ask him to deal with the guy. I think he would talk to him, but this guy just wouldn't adjust. He could not see me as a classmate.

Chad: Mm.

Carol: I was always a sexual object to him. So, one time, he said, "You know, we oughta hang out Saturday night." And I just said, "Okay. Come and pick me up at such-and-such time." I just called his bluff on it. And that kind of got him straight.

As the only Black in class, I couldn't be absent, because it would be readily known to the professor. The classes were not that large. And the people I really got to know in those classes were the people in my study group, and Armando was always the closest one to me. I chose to stay in the dorm that was majority African-American. I remember getting to Stanford and meeting with the other students and realizing how many of them had gone to private school.

Chad: What is the cultural climate in the sciences and academia for you as a Black woman? How has that changed, if at all, over the last twenty, thirty years of your career?

Carol: When I left Stanford I went to MIT. That's a very intimidating environment. I joined this research group that had never had a woman and they had never had an African-American. There were grad students who didn't like the fact that I was there, but there were others who treated me like an equal. But it was tough. And there were things that should have been shared with me that weren't, like the library of algorithms that had been developed to do various types of signal processing. I was there for several months writing from scratch the code for the algorithms I needed because I didn't know this library existed. That cost me a lot of time. I learned that the graduate student who helped to manage the lab was the person who should have told me about this library.

There were definitely microaggressions. I had a professor

there who would not even say hi to me unless other people were around. But if we were walking toward each other in the hallway, he would look away rather than speak to me. That was definitely intimidating because this was someone who was very well known and had a lot of power. I felt that maybe I had done something or had not done something that was protocol. I discussed it with some other Black grad students and decided to meet with the professor. He encouraged me to leave MIT and go to Georgia Tech. That was a lot.

I knew the story about my dad and I decided I was not going to give this man the power to decide my fate. And that's where my spiritual upbringing really kicked in. It was a tough decision to make to stay there, given the amount of microaggressions going on. But what that professor did was blatant. I just decided that God loved me as much as he loves anybody else and that he could be in rooms and make things happen, even though I might not even know these conversations are going on. But I trusted that if I stayed the course and did what I was supposed to and put in the time, everything would come to fruition. And it did.

I ended up switching to a different research group in part to avoid the professor. This group had a lot of women in it. Again, I was the only Black, but there were other women because it was a very interdisciplinary group. So that was just night and day. I hadn't realized how stressed I was until I joined there and then I kind of went: [exhales] breath of fresh air. I hadn't realized I was so oppressed in the other group.

Once I got my PhD, I ran into that one professor at a conference. It was all fine. He acted like none of that had ever happened.

Chad: Mm.

Carol: I knew that I wanted to be a professor. I had enjoyed doing research—even though maybe the research group that I was initially a part of was hard to be a part of. And I did not want to go into industry at that time. You can imagine, Chad, if you found it very tense at Google, what it was like at that point. I had done summers at companies and man, you know, I was always made to feel like a stranger or a guest in that environment. I was constantly minoritized.

Chad: Yeah.

Carol: So I went to grad school and realized I enjoyed teaching. When I found out I really liked the research aspect of it, then I was like, "Yes, this is something. This is my calling. I am supposed to be doing this." I wasn't going to let this guy take that away from me because I would always look back and say, "What if I had stayed?" I don't want to have regrets like that, where you give somebody control to make you switch to something else.

I ended up doing well. You know, there were other hurdles. Believe me, there were definitely other hurdles at MIT. It's not an easy place. My husband began his career at MIT by conducting an interview-based research study of the experiences of Black students. One student spoke for many when he said MIT is a good place to be from but not a good place to be at.

Being in STEM and being a woman in STEM and being African-American in STEM, you just have to get comfortable with being uncomfortable. Because you're not going to see a lot of people around you that look like you. And that does have an effect on the quality of your life. But if you are doing what you are really called to do, you learn to deal with the other stuff. You know? And you carve your world.

Being a professor is like doing PR. You've gotta present at a lot of conferences, and for many years I went to conferences and I didn't see another Black person. It's getting better—not a whole lot better—but it's better than when I first started out. And again, that's a situation where you have to learn to be comfortable with being uncomfortable. I used to hate going to conferences for that reason, because the jokes that were told weren't funny to me. The things people liked doing weren't things that I would choose to do on my own, because it wasn't my culture.

Chad: Right.

Carol: You still have to keep at it. You still have to go to these things. You start to meet people who you actually develop friendships with and collaborate with and it changes. So, now, going to conferences is not such a big deal to me. In fact, some of them I look forward to because I'm going to see colleagues from different universities. But it took a while to get that level of comfort. You have to achieve. You had to prove yourself. People see you doing good work and you are supporting students and you're raising money and you're holding your own. That attracts people and they're more your equals. No one's looking down or thinking any kind of special thing has been done. That's the thing that irks me the most: times when people think you're getting special favors because you're African-American or a woman. When it's just the opposite. You know, the conversations work against you, not for you. In my day, people frowned upon you doing work with other people. They wanted to see that you, on your own, could raise money to support yourself and to support your grad students and your laboratories. And I was really successful. I got a lot of National Science Foundation grants and I had quite a few grad students. I was told that in a meeting, someone said, "Well, she probably got those because she's Black."

Chad: Right.

Carol: They were all the mainstream grants that everybody competed for. Nobody knows when you're doing it that you're Black. I mean, unless they already know you because they worked with you. But they're reading the proposals and making the decisions based on what's written in your proposals and the previous work you did and how successful you were with that. And they could see that I was getting money from the standard programs. These were not any special programs. But they still make the comment anyway, you know what I'm saying? You just have to let that roll off of you. And just move on.

Chad: Mmhmm.

Carol: They wouldn't have said it if it was a white male, and he had the same list of grants that I had with the same titles from the same programs—nobody would have said anything.

Chad: If a young person picks up this book and flips to your chapter, is there any one message you'd want her to have about how to feel strong and prideful in her cultural upbringing as she starts her career?

Carol: You need to understand history. Some of that you have to do on your own because I doubt if American high schools are providing that yet. Definitely not in my day. But colleges usually have really good African-American Studies departments now, and I think it's very important to understand your history. If you understand your history, you should be really proud. There is nothing to be ashamed of about our trajectory. And the fact that we are still surviving here in the US is really remarkable. I think it really speaks to the strength of our ancestors, right? You just need to understand the truth. There are a lot of books out there that tell lies in them, or don't have us in them at all. Or they cover us very little. But you can get the information now.

Understand ancient civilizations and understand what is going on in Africa as well as the Middle Passage and slavery. If you understand that, you should derive strength that should make you want to excel more. Because so many people sacrificed so that future generations would have opportunities that they didn't have. I think we have a very proud history. I'm not ashamed of anything in our history.

Chapter Four

WORK

"At the most basic we are only discussing a learned skill, but do we not agree that sometimes the most basic skills can create things far beyond our expectations? We are talking about tools and carpentry, about words and style . . . but as we move along, you'd do well to remember that we are also talking about magic."

—Stephen King

━━━━━━━━▶◆◆◆◆◆◀━━━━━━━━

I wasn't sure what I would do after I finished my senior year at Morehouse with an English degree. I took the LSAT but didn't want to go to law school. My summer internships at the NAACP, NBA, and Teach for America didn't demonstrate a particular skill set. Teach for America offered me a teaching position, but I worried I didn't have the patience for that extremely important job. Days before I was going to accept the offer from TFA, I met a Black Google recruiter visiting Morehouse. Her name was LaFawn Bailey, and after forty-five minutes of chatting with her in The Caf, she asked if I'd like to officially apply for an entry level job at Google.

"Do I have to wear a suit?" I asked.

"No," she laughed. "Wear whatever you want." Perfect.

LaFawn and a white recruiter named Angela interviewed me in an empty Morehouse classroom. The conversation was casual. They asked about my extracurriculars and the holes in my transcript. They asked what I wanted from my career, and my life. I must have come off as pretty naive when it was my turn to ask questions.

"So what exactly does Google *do*?" I asked. They were kind enough not to laugh at me. It seemed like something I should know if I was going to work there. But they smiled.

"We make money by selling advertisements on the search results you get when you *Google* something," Angela said. That made sense. *Kinda*. I nodded.

"But we have dozens of products as a company. Search is just our bread and butter."

My nod must have been sufficient because they moved on. I felt like I'd done okay in the interview. A few days later, I received an email inviting me to Google's Mountain View headquarters in Silicon Valley for on-campus interviews.

I arrived at Google's headquarters and took in what looked like a McDonald's PlayPlace for grown-ups. The buildings featured Google's iconic blue, red, green, and yellow color scheme, smattered with solar panels. Early models of self-driving cars buzzed around the lots. Employees on bicycles rode at a leisurely pace from building to building. Others lay on grass nearby. I was led by a young, bubbly white recruiter through a micro-kitchen stocked with organic fruits and salads, cereals, sandwich spreads, soda fountains, water bottles, ice cream cones, and candy. I saw chefs cooking in the open-faced kitchens in front of a cafeteria.

"Grab something," the recruiter instructed. "You're gonna be in back-to-back meetings for like three hours."

I had no appetite. I was in awe of the entire situation—and I had to stay focused. I had been given next to no information on what I would be asked in my interviews. I grabbed a flavored water bottle and a granola bar to be polite.

We took the stairs up to the fourth floor, passing a friendly off-leash Labrador retriever walking beside a tall, white man in his forties—his owner, I figured. The man was stubbly and nerdy-handsome with a protruding Adam's apple. His name was probably Adam, I thought. The man and my host spoke, then he turned to me.

"Hey, how's it going, buddy?" Adam said.

I paused. Then I said: "Umm, hey, I'm pretty good." It hit me that I had almost forgotten how to talk to white guys. I hadn't forgotten what to say, but how to say it. Chin up, back stiff, handshake at a perfect ninety-degree angle, no chest or shoulder contact. Never mind the way we'd pull each other into a hug at Morehouse. I was awkward, but Adam didn't notice. His eyes focused straight ahead over a three-quarters smile. I felt a distance of a million miles between us but he *looked* so happy. That sort of empty, plastered smile embodied what I'd learn to be the required company expression. That was *Googliness.*

My host dropped me off in a small conference room. The room was uninteresting except for its plainness, which starkly contrasted with the rest of the colorful campus. On the desk were a Google-branded pen and notepad. I gathered that those were for me.

I sat for a beat tapping the pen on the notepad until the

door swung open and a white man with Warby Parker glasses and floppy black hair bounded into the room.

"Aw, hey dude, welcome," he said. "I'm Tom!"

Hi, Tom!

Ninety-degree handshake. No chest or shoulder contact. Tom pulled out a scoring rubric and laid it on the table. Later, I'd learn that the rubric consisted of several mundane scoring areas—mental aptitude, job-related skills, basic understanding of concepts—and one more complicated area: the aforementioned *Googliness*. This was where the interviewer was to judge the interviewee on whether or not he was someone the interviewer would want to work with; to see every day in the micro-kitchen; to pet his dog in the stairway; to share ninety-degree handshakes.

I knew without seeing the scoring rubric that I would be judged first on whether or not I made Tom feel comfortable. I was rusty when it came to this, but I had a deep well of experience in mostly white classrooms to draw from. Those years taught me to smile big, use words like "bro" and "dude," raise the sound of my voice a quarter octave, and laugh at anything that smelled like a joke. Someone who didn't know these social cues might sadly be deemed . . . not *Googly*.

"So it says here you go to Morehouse," Tom said. "Now, that's in Kentucky, right?"

"No, that's Morehead." I'd heard that one before. I corrected him with an unthreatening smile.

"Hah! Sorry," Tom said. "Got my Mores wrong."

He laughed. *Hah! Haha! HAHAHA! FUNNY!* I laughed to make him feel good about his joke and ignorance.

"Morehouse. That's an HBCU right?"

"Yep."

"So how's *that*?" Tom asked. He looked at me like I'd said I went to school on a remote island without water or electricity.

"Oh, I love it," I said. "Best decision I've ever made." I stopped myself from saying more. I could have said it was so refreshing to have my self-esteem rebuilt in the safety of an HBCU and that I thanked God I didn't go to my second choice—an Ivy League—where I may have had my voice trampled in racially isolating classrooms. That might not come across as Googly. Tom tilted his head and nodded.

"Okay, nice. Well let's get started," he said.

I remember the first two questions he asked.

Question one: Given one hour and unlimited resources, what's the fastest way to find a needle in a haystack?

Question two: There are two skyscrapers separated by one hundred meters. Your task is to walk a tightrope from the top of one to the top of the other with proof of completion and without falling. How would you execute this?

My answer to question one was to push the haystack into a small, inflatable pool. Once the hay floated to the surface, I would scrape the pool's bottom for the needle. I never got around to a real answer on question 2. I would never tightrope between skyscrapers.

That night, I flew back to Atlanta. I headed straight to a North Atlanta club called the Velvet Room for a senior week party without even stopping at home to change clothes. I didn't think much about my interview at Google. I had a very important schedule of cookouts, pre-games, and parties to tend to. Days later, I received an offer from Google inviting me to join their organization as part of its People Operations Division at the Mountain View headquarters. I didn't think I was Googly, but I accepted because I wanted to be.

◆ ◆

People Operations was a glamorous name for Human Resources. My job often felt like busywork, but the company's size and power intrigued me. So I did my job well enough to remain employed. I stayed for four years.

In those years I moved around between roles. I started in the Mountain View, California, headquarters, then transferred to New York, then to London and then back to New York. Looking back, I appreciate that the company gave me the opportunity to jump around until I found where I fit. That was in London. Something about being away from my home country made me feel like I could express myself more honestly. I felt less of the weight of racial expectations from my colleagues, who were mostly British, French, Spanish, and Australian. I spoke from my own voice, rather than the constricting bipolarity of speaking "like a Black person" or "like a white person." I was just myself, which included being effortlessly, essentially Black.

It was then that I thrived. I took on greater projects, I was given larger budgets, I was granted permission to travel to other countries to lead initiatives, I managed important relationships with external partners and big universities. Suddenly, I had a trajectory, and it took three years for me to realize that I needed to be myself to have any success in this confusing company.

In my first year, I used the restroom in one of the Mountain View campus's many restaurants, in a building I'd never visited. When I tried to exit the bathroom, I realized I was locked inside. I pulled as hard as I could on the door and it didn't budge. I pushed my foot up against the wall and I pulled even harder. CLANK. I fell on the floor, handle in hand. The door gently swung open in the opposite direction. I was pulling on the wrong side of the door.

There stood Google cofounder Sergey Brin, net worth $50 billion. He was wearing those awful wet shoes with the individual toes. I scrambled to my feet. I rushed to apologize. He just smiled at me. That distant, plastered, Googly expression. He proceeded to one of the urinals. I left the handle on the floor and exited as quickly as I could.

Before that moment, I had only seen Sergey on stage in front of thousands at company conferences. He seemed like a superhero then, like Iron Man. But here he was just a guy who had to pee. I realized while standing beside him that human beings built Google. *Google.* The place that revolutionized the tech industry. The place that had its own twenty-four-hour mainstream media news cycle. The place that employed hundreds of thousands of people since 1998, when it was founded in a Palo Alto garage. This guy and his friend Larry Page built that. And, again, here he was. Just a person who had to pee.

I wanted what he had: wealth, power, freedom—to create, to wear terrible wet shoes around an office that belonged to me, whatever. I'd always wanted those things, but I had pushed my dreams down deep to focus on work I didn't care much about so I could keep my job.

When I was a kid, my dad told me stories about entrepreneurs who started businesses that led them to wealth. Both of my grandfathers were entrepreneurs after serving in the army. One built a shoe repair business in Maryland, the other owned a dry-cleaning business in Detroit. Neither became rich, but entrepreneurialism was part of our family. We openly discussed the risks associated. In his forties, my dad started his own law practice, which gave him the flexibility to be a present father.

As a child, when I became obsessed with products like Super Nintendo, McDonald's, Nickelodeon, the NBA, my dad challenged me to learn how each thing came to be. He reminded me that everything I liked and everything I saw started as someone's idea. Someone just like me. When my dad noticed me playing Xbox for three hours without a break in my bedroom on a Saturday, he went down to his home office and reemerged with a stack of printed papers. He turned off my gaming system and dropped thirty pages in my lap.

"Here's everything you need to know about the people who created the Xbox and how they did it," he said. "When you finish reading, I'm going to quiz you. If you pass, you can turn your game back on. If you fail, the game stays off."

I got in the habit of learning how things were built and who built them. I read about their bankruptcies caused by their money problems while taking on the risk to build. There were loan defaults, divorces, and destroyed families. But the lucky ones eventually struck gold with a product or service that found a market. I imagine the ones who died as failures were never written about, so I can't say much about them.

Eventually I started to enjoy studying how those entrepreneurs survived the risk period long enough to find success. I read writers like Tim Ferriss, who chronicled the paths of the world's great creators, which helped me track their journeys. A pattern emerged: many who were able to achieve success and wealth in business had to suffer short-term discomforts to do so. Oprah. Milton Hershey. Steve Jobs. Jay-Z. Those people are so fabled in capitalist America that they feel more like superheroes than people.

Seeing Sergey that day made the dream feel attainable. But I was too scared to try to build something of my own. I had a job at a company that many people wanted to work for. I was making pretty good money for someone my age, with free food and unlimited sick days. So I stayed. But I cringed each time I read about another venture capital–backed tech startup run by twenty-somethings selling to a big tech company like Google. It made me feel small. Why didn't I have the courage to shoot my shot?

In 2011 Snapchat popped up. Then Lyft in 2012. Slack in 2013, just to name a few of hundreds. I was watching them closely from my company-issued MacBook in my cubicle. I told myself it was easier for white guys to get funding. I listened to friends and mentors who said I should sit still and be grateful for the job I had. I made up excuses to rationalize my fear of risk taking.

But I didn't sleep well at night. I felt like I was *supposed* to go out on my own and build something. The voices in my head were telling me that every day and night. I tried to dull those voices with social media, partying, more open tabs on my laptop, more Google docs crammed with ideas and business plans that I never got around to, more travel, more "work," more happy hour, more Coachella, more dating, more whatever. But whenever there was a break in my schedule of inconsequential bullshitting, the voices returned.

In 2014, four years after I started at Google, I jumped on as an early employee at a small tech startup that offered nineteen-week boot camps to teach career changers how to code. I joined as a partner and eventually became head of business development. But I wasn't a founder. It wasn't *mine*. When the company sold to Kaplan a few years later, my lack of ownership was reflected in my tiny share of equity outpay. I received a check for less than $2,000. It was a nominal pat on the ass. I had been part of building something, but I didn't take the real risk. The founders did that. And they were rewarded for doing so. The voices were still telling me to do something on my own.

But starting something on my own meant being alone. I was hiding from that because I had been "alone" before, in all those classrooms, and all those bonfire house parties, and honors assemblies, and magnet school buses. I didn't want to feel that again. That kind of isolation scared me.

And yet, the voices.

I finally quit my job because Kaplan bought our company. I didn't want to be a small drop in a giant bucket, again, as I had been at Google. I joined my mentor Ed—the Black executive I looked up to when I started at Google—and worked as a consultant. He was in California and I was in Brooklyn. The checks from our work were rare and spare.

I had no other coworkers, no insurance of any kind, no direct deposit, no strings attached to any corporation to buoy me. Now it was just me and a three-hundred-square-foot studio apartment, big enough for me and a couch *or* bed, but not both. I'd go to the bars and coffee shops near my apartment and order the cheapest tea on the menu just to use the wifi and be around people. My days were maddeningly quiet. The same cell phone I had used to distract myself from uninteresting workdays hardly rang now. It just sat there. The recruiters who used to swirl to poach me when I worked at Google disappeared. My old colleagues at the tech startup, who I thought were close friends, turned out to just be work friends. Most of them disappeared faster than the recruiters.

I watched my savings deplete. I was living in New York, one of the most expensive cities in the world, and the bills mounted. I had to make decisions to cut off small expenses that hardly made a dent before, when I had a reliable income. My Netflix subscription. My Spotify account. That might sound trivial, but going months without music or TV created a very uncomfortable silence. I stopped checking the mail, to avoid the bills. I needed to find a way to make real money, fast. I was without health insurance, meaning any significant illness or accident would have been disastrous. I was constantly on edge.

But I was also exhilarated. The loneliness I felt reminded me of the kind I felt growing up in class, but the familiarity triggered coping devices I developed back then. As a kid I had to block out the voices of judgment I felt from my peers and teachers so I could hear my own voice and make decisions.

My classroom disposition swung between anxious charm, distracted detachment, and seething disdain for my classmates and teachers. But in English class I transformed. When it was time to read our own work aloud, I had control of the room. I *knew* my experience and voice were unique even if only because I was Black. I leaned into my racial differences in my writing instead of trying to hide them. I was willing to pander to whiteness in person, even if it made me feel shameful. But it felt impossible to be dishonest on the page. I don't mean that figuratively. I tried to be more palatable to whiteness in my writing, but it made me feel queasy.

As a teen, alone as I was, I could retreat to the page with my unfiltered thoughts and feelings. I escaped isolation in writing.

So when I was living in a tiny apartment, nearly broke and very alone, I went back to what I knew. I tried to write myself out of isolation. Writing was my instinctive coping mechanism for isolation. And because I needed money, I wondered if I could make some money doing it.

I decided to write a screenplay for a TV show based on my own life. From there, I thought, I'd try to sell the show to a network. I had no idea how to do that. It was an improbable and naive idea. But in my isolation, there was nobody around to tell me not to try.

I had no experience screenwriting. But I just started writing from the gut, steering into honesty about race. That's what I had done in high school. I'd written about feeling crushed under whiteness, to expunge and organize my feelings. It was therapy then. Now I had Issa Rae's *Insecure* and Donald Glover's *Atlanta* as inspiration. They were young Black people who'd created their own shows somewhat based on their lives. Why couldn't I?

I had the benefit of *no one*. No mentor to tell me to pay my dues and climb the ranks by getting coffee for someone else or working in the mailroom at an agency. There were no academics to tell me to go get a master of fine arts degree at NYU. I had no writing partner to lean on or hide behind. Just four walls and a MacBook and a stack of bills and the voices in my head.

Off I went. Isolation and urgency formed a powder keg. Many Black people have large quantities of both, and I believe it can serve as the necessity that breeds creativity and sales instincts.

◆ ◆

"BEEN BROKE BEFORE." My friend Quincy Avery, who I interview later in this book, sometimes wears a T-shirt displaying this message in big capital letters partially covered by his thick, black, sailor's beard. Today, Quincy is flown around the world to train NFL quarterbacks. Eight years ago, Quincy was living in his car, chasing down QB prospects on Twitter to train them for free so that he could turn those relationships into real business later. Quincy was homeless, but he was never hopeless. Quincy was just as joyful then, driving between Atlanta to LA in his used SUV, as he is now, flying first class from Ohio State to Houston to stand on the sidelines with his clients and make ESPN appearances. Quincy relishes the idea that he went for broke and cashed in. We Americans love a rags-to-riches story. Walt Disney and Milton Hershey (of Hershey's Chocolate) filed for bankruptcy multiple times before making their fortunes. FUBU founder Daymond John wrote an entire book, *The Power of Broke*, celebrating the lessons of resourcefulness and urgency he learned from being hungry with a tight budget. We love the idea that someone with "nothing" can create wealth with resilience and imagination. It gives us hope. And a pleasant distraction from the fact that the vast majority of us are born and die without changing tax brackets.

Being broke that year in New York taught me that living lean could push me to make use of my innate resources: creativity, relationships, and independent thinking.

I was very afraid. As a Black man I realized then that I equated money and a "good job" with safety. Safety from wrongful incrimination. Safety from the police. Safety from being a statistic. Money represented legal fees if ever I should need them. Money represented healthcare. Money represented an ability to provide; money was manhood and attractiveness.

A part of what was scary about being broke was that I'm not even *that guy*. I was never the guy who flaunted money to appear strong. I never wore a chain or drove a flashy car. I rarely bought trendy, expensive sneakers. I never even knew what was trendy enough to be worth buying to show people that I had money when I had some. I was always so proud of being *the other guy*. I was the asshole judging from my perch on high; looking down and laughing.

"I don't really like things, I prefer to pay for *experiences*." I was that guy. That guy is the worst.

And then I became an entrepreneur, a writer, and I became broke.

I didn't grow up broke. My parents were gainfully employed, graduate-degreed professionals. Also, there were two of them in our one house, which was a sizable advantage most of my friends didn't have. We had books everywhere. We had TVs on all three floors of our house. We had a refrigerator full of food and art on the walls and a piano and photos in picture frames.

"Chad's family has money" is what I later learned some of my friends said about us.

We were middle-class. My mom drove a Volvo, my dad drove an Acura. I was twenty-four the first time I left the country. I knew that my dad had grown up without much money, that he and his brother shared a fold-away bed in the kitchen in their small house in Detroit.

I knew that we weren't wealthy because I watched *The Fresh Prince of Bel-Air*. Money mattered in our house in a way that it didn't to the Banks family. We were closer to *Family Matters*. *Maybe* the Huxtables.

My closest friendships were with the players on my all-Black basketball teams growing up. They're still my closest friends today. Many of their families had less money and were captained by single mothers working hard to make rent in apartments and houses they didn't own. Sometimes the electricity would go out for days because of overdue bills. There were few if any books in the house. There were robberies here and there. There was usually very little food in the fridge, but there was Kool-Aid.

On the weekends my boys would work odd jobs. They'd umpire Little League baseball games or valet cars to get cash. I always wondered why they spent their time that way. I was privileged and ignorant. They needed the money for school lunch or dollar menu items at McDonald's and Jordan sneakers to look like they had more money than they did.

I remember one time I walked with a couple of my boys to the 7-Eleven convenience store ten minutes up the road from our high school. There was a lunchtime crowd of students, mostly white kids spending money their parents gave them on Slurpies, cigarettes, and condoms. The three of us all walked in together, Black kids in hoodies. I followed my two buddies around the store until I noticed them grabbing items from the stocked shelves and pocketing them. It was the first time I realized my friends stole. I ran outside of the store when it dawned on me. I was terrified of being caught and having to face my parents.

I stood all the way across the street, staring at the store. I became angry. I judged my friends. Why would they risk getting arrested and going to jail for pizza-flavored Doritos? I watched them walk out the front door, unnoticed.

We started the walk together down New Hampshire Avenue toward our high school. We were halfway there before one of them addressed my silence.

"What's your problem, Boulder?" the taller one said. The other chuckled, munching on Doritos.

"He's mad cus we stole," he said.

They knew me well. The friend who spoke up knew I was judging them for "corner-cutting." After all, I had the two-parent house with the big yard and books and food and snacks everywhere. I was the one always complaining about white people exploiting their privilege, while completely ignoring my own.

"Y'all are tripping," I said. "You're gonna get caught and go to jail." They laughed at me.

"Why don't y'all just get lunch at school?" I continued.

"That shit is way overpriced," one friend replied.

It was the first time I ever even *considered* the price of lunch at school. My entire life I mindlessly paid the cost of school lunch with money my parents gave me. I thought my friends were stealing from the 7-Eleven to look cool or because school food was gross. They were doing it because they were hungry and the school food was unaffordable.

They were broke, or close to it. As such, they learned how to manage their time and money as fifteen-year-olds. They became entrepreneurs. One downloaded every new rap album on Napster and burned CDs to sell at school for $10, usually making ten- to twenty-times profit margins on the cheap blank CDs he'd buy at Target. Another, a talented visual artist, would draw beautiful designs of popular cartoon characters with cheap fabric pens on $5 black T-shirts, selling them for $30 to $40. Babysitters. Dog walkers. You name it, my friends would find a way to make money. They'd save up for months to buy clothes, video game consoles, gifts for their mothers and younger siblings. To this day, they're still more thoughtful financial planners and budgeters than me.

They were hustling. I'd float in and out, observing and wondering why they were so into their hobbies that they'd skip a big party Friday night to wake up early and get to the baseball diamond to umpire for $25 the next morning. It wasn't until a decade later, when *I* was broke, that I understood. I followed their blueprint to recognize what I had that I could sell. That turned out to be my writing.

They knew as teenagers that they needed to make money to eat. They were unfazed by that truth. It was normal and they adapted a skill set to account for it.

In 2010, the median wealth for Black families was $4,900 compared to $97,000 for white families. We're broke. At the very least, many of us have *been broke before*. If you've been broke before, you too may have found inventive ways to use your resources to feed yourself. That's creative. That's why it's called *making* money. That's magic.

◆ ◆

I spent one month writing my TV pilot. I didn't have time to spare with New York bills piling up. And thank God, because I might still be writing that damn pilot if I'd had a trust fund to fall back on. I was writing the last ten pages of my pilot at a coffee shop in Fort Greene when I decided to take a break. I had leaned over to stretch when I saw a Black man in his fifties wearing funky thick red-framed glasses and Jordan sneakers. He was unmistakable. It was Spike Lee, legendary filmmaker and Morehouse alumnus. He was sitting alone, scrolling on a BlackBerry phone. We were just forty feet away from his 40 Acres & a Mule Filmworks studio headquarters. I didn't think. I walked over to introduce myself.

"Hey, Mr. Lee. I'm . . ."

"Call me Spike."

"Okay, Mr. Spike. I'm Chad Sanders. I went to Morehouse and I . . ."

"Morehouse man! What's up brother?"

He gave me a dap and a hug. Morehouse protocol.

"Tell me, what's going on my Morehouse brother?" he said.

"I just saw you sitting here and I thought I should introduce myself. I just quit my job a couple months ago and I'm working on some new things . . . ," I said.

"Yeah? What are you working on?" he asked.

I told him everything about me *except* that I was writing a TV show. I thought it wasn't ready. I thought I wasn't ready. I thought he was too important to care. The man created *Malcolm X*, one of my favorite movies ever; a film that etched race into my brain as a child. *Do the Right Thing. 25th Hour. School Daze. He Got Game.* Why would he want to read a half-done script by a first-timer who didn't go to film school? So I told him I used to work at Google. I thought that would be impressive. I told him about the tech startup. When I started boring him, he gave me his email address and sent me on my way.

Over the next month I finished the TV pilot and shared it with a couple close friends, as well as former Morehouse College president Dr. John Wilson. Dr. Wilson had officiated my sister's wedding, and when he asked me what I was up to, I told him about the TV pilot. I was embarrassed to say I was unemployed and without a plan for the next phase of my life. Dr. Wilson mentioned that he and Spike had been friends since they were students at Morehouse together. He encouraged me to share my work, but even then, I couldn't bring myself to email Spike Lee. I sent the screenplay to Dr. Wilson but not Spike.

Weeks later, I was sitting in my barber's chair in Bed Stuy when my phone rang. It was an unrecognized number with a New York area code. I answered.

"Hello?"

"Yo, this is Spike."

"Who?"

"This is Spike Lee! Listen, I got your screenplay from John Wilson. It's good. Here's what I want you to do . . . meet me at 40 Acres & a Mule Filmworks in Fort Greene on Saturday at 9 p.m. See you soon, my Morehouse brother."

I couldn't believe it. I checked the number a few times. I thought it was one of my friends playing a prank on me. But it wasn't. That night, when I knelt to pray before bed, I thanked God for the call from Spike. I thought I should pray for something to come out of my meeting with him, but I didn't even know what to ask for. I knew so little about Hollywood and show business.

On Saturday, I walked into the bottom level of the 40 Acres & a Mule Filmworks studio. Iconic art and framed artifacts were all over the walls: Michael Jackson's red jacket, Prince's purple and gold boots, Michael Jordan's game-worn shoes, Tina Turner's microphone, a poster of *The Departed* signed by

Martin Scorsese. In the center of the room was a long, wooden table big enough to fit twenty people. Seated alone at the head of the table was Spike. In front of him was my TV pilot. Spike had marked up every page in red.

"Sit down, my Morehouse brother!" he directed.

I did as I was told. Spike walked me through every page of my screenplay. Our conversation was balanced. He never forced a note on me, and he listened carefully if I pushed back on any of his suggestions. I wanted to endear myself to him, but I felt defensive of my work because it had come from such a personal place. It wasn't until after I left that night that I realized I had just debated notes with Spike Lee on my first screenplay.

When he turned the final page, Spike pulled out a small, white index card and scrawled on it in red ink.

"Strong Move To Da Hoop," he wrote at the top of the index card. He then listed four prominent networks that would be suitable homes for *our* show.

"We'll fly to Los Angeles next Monday and pitch together. We'll take the red-eye back to New York that night," he said. "Text me your address. There will be a car for you at 5 a.m. to take you to the airport."

I was in shock. Me and Spike Lee became creative partners in a matter of weeks. But first, I had to be alone. I had to actually sit down and dig and find the story inside me.

"You're a writer, my Morehouse brother," he reminded me. "This is what you do."

My voice as a writer comes from being alone for so many years with my own thoughts, squished and compressed by all-encompassing, suffocating whiteness. Nearly all the business leaders and entrepreneurs featured in this book talked about this feeling. But there's a gift that comes with it: You spend time with your thoughts. You talk to yourself. You find your truest, strongest convictions because you know every word that you speak or put down on paper will be scrutinized and batted around.

My high school basketball coach—the one who changed my life by sending me home to change into a collared shirt before my Morehouse interview—played college ball for Hampton University. He used to run our practices without a whistle. He said he wanted us to be able to identify and respond to his voice when we played in hostile and loud environments. I lost my ability to identify my own voice when I worked in the noise of droning pleasantries, Googliness, and busywork in corporate America. But when I was jobless, afraid, and isolated in that tiny apartment, I started to hear my voice again. My phone wasn't ringing anymore and my friends were busy with their own lives in their own jobs at corporations. All I could hear was my own voice. That voice led me back to my writing and that writing led me to Spike Lee. Spike Lee led me to a career.

◆ ◆

Spike and I pitched the show all over Hollywood, breaking down the story of a young, Black genius whose life was turned inside out by the unexpected success of his pet project—a dating app that read sexual chemistry. We planned to shoot a ten-episode first season with a largely Black cast in Brooklyn.

Each pitch resembled the last. We'd walk into a chic meeting room with a large white table in the center, surrounded by framed photos of the network's most successful shows. Two or three executives greeted us at the door with broad smiles and firm handshakes. Sometimes a younger executive in her mid-twenties would join as well.

Before we embarked, Spike explained that we would hear many nos. He told me to remember that every no just got us closer to a yes.

"This business is about failure, my Morehouse brother," he reminded me between our first two pitches. "It doesn't matter if nine doors close in our faces as long as the tenth door opens."

I didn't accept that the business was about failure even when he told me so plainly. I thought that with someone like Spike attached to my project, networks would be beating my door down to buy *Archer*.

Once inside and seated, the top-ranking exec would make a joke to lead off a three- to five-minute round of pleasantries. He'd make eye contact with Spike throughout the meeting and barely look at me.

"So, I imagine you've done a couple of these," the exec would say to Spike with Hollywood bravado. The exec would flash a $10,000 watch and cuff links engraved with his initials. Sometimes Spike was willing to play ball.

"Once or twice," Spike would respond, in his way. Then he would quickly launch into our pitch.

"So my Morehouse brother is here today with a brilliant show he created," Spike would say, selling both the show and me. "Tell them who you are and tell them about the show, brother."

I'd introduce myself, describing the road that led me from Silver Spring to their conference rooms. Then I'd segue into an overview of the show, its characters and my partnership with Spike, detailing our vision for why the show was timely and how it would resonate with audiences between twenty-five and forty, especially people of color. I tried to emulate Spike's detached confidence to overcompensate for nerves.

The executives seemed enthralled by the concept. They said it was edgy, modern, and fresh, heads nodding and calling other execs in to listen to the premise. They'd ask their questions. Did I have any ideas for casting? What shows could I compare this to? What sort of budget would we need to execute this vision?

The meeting would wrap after twenty-five minutes followed by a round of handshakes. Spike and I would head back down to the lobby to prepare for the next meeting.

"You're good at this," Spike reassured me in the car after the third pitch. "Trust yourself. This is going very well, my young brother."

After what felt like the most promising pitch, my mom called to check on our progress. Spike said he wanted to answer.

"Hello, this is Spike! I just wanna tell you your son is a genius! We're 'bout to make a TV show."

My mom, who'd attended Spelman College while Spike was at Morehouse, still holds on to that phone call. She was very worried when I decided to leave tech and become a writer of all things. Spike's phone call reassured her. I was grateful to him for that.

Each meeting, the pitch felt stronger than the last. The laughs were louder, the questions more thoughtful, the smiles wider. But every single meeting would catch on one snag. The execs wanted to know how our show differed from HBO's *Silicon Valley*.

Silicon Valley follows the journey of five khaki-shorts-wearing, computer-game-playing tech bro nerds building a startup in Silicon Valley. Four white guys in rumpled hoodies

and a Pakistani guy. The primary conflict of the story is whether
these tech bros will become wealthy or just rich. The show looks
and feels authentic to the Silicon Valley tech bro culture, which
is one reason it has been successful . . . and why I couldn't watch
beyond season 2. Watching it made me feel as excluded from
the techy good ol' boys club as I felt when I worked in Silicon
Valley. I'd already spent four years watching Stanford frat bros
in hoodies and crocs fall up. I didn't need to spend more time
reminiscing.

I thought it was obvious: a show about a young Black entrepreneur learning to cope with success was a different story.
I was wrong. I tried to explain that a Black person's journey
through the worlds of venture capital and condescending Wall
Streeters without a white safety net made for a completely
different—higher stakes—journey than *Silicon Valley*. Either
I didn't communicate that message well or the execs found it
unmarketable.

Responses from networks trickled in through our agents.
Each network turned down my show in a stream of vaguely
worded emails. All I could decipher from the industry jargon was that my show felt like "*Silicon Valley* for Black people." From my point of view, there is no such thing as "White
Thing X for Black people." Race is too meaningful to just
throw Black characters into an existing format and label it "for
Black people." The dimensions of our worlds are completely
different. Life's simplest experiences, like walking home with
an Arizona Iced Tea and routine traffic stops, carry life-or-
death stakes.

I went back to my agents and scrambled to set up a few more
pitches for the show. My bank account was close to empty. I'd

spent most of my money flying back and forth to Hollywood for meetings, crashing on friends' couches. (Thank you, Justin and Taylor. Thank you, Leon and Kristin.) I was scared. My friends were buying houses, having kids, getting promoted in safe corporate gigs, filling up their 401(k)s. I was missing weddings and baby showers because I couldn't afford to travel there while I was schlepping back and forth across the country for pitch meetings. My absence was affecting my friendships and I feared being left behind.

I called Spike. I told him I was afraid of what might happen to me if I wasn't able to find a network partner. I had no writing credits, no industry track record. I had jumped ship on a tech career that provided me stability. I was so close to asking to borrow money from Spike, but I was too proud to go through with it.

He must have heard the panic in my voice. His response stays with me.

"This is a tough industry but you're built for this. This is what you do. You're a writer, and because of that you will never struggle to feed yourself. If you ever need me to remind you of that, anytime, call me. Just not at 2 a.m."

Damn. It wasn't afternoon. It was 2 *a.m.* I'd lost track of time, freaking out in my apartment with the blinds drawn. But in this moment where it felt like the walls were closing in on me, his vote of confidence gave me fuel to try again.

Spike had to start shooting his film *BlacKkKlansman*, so I attended my final pitch alone. It was at BET. Everything felt different from my previous meetings. Basquiat paintings lined the walls. All the executives and staff I met were Black. We spent the first fifteen minutes of our conversation talking about the state of Hollywood for Black people. When I launched into the pitch, the executives followed closely. They related to the complexity of a young Black person forging his way in a hot industry. Every now and then, an "mmm" or a "yeah, I feel that."

The words *Silicon Valley* were never uttered as a comparison. They just . . . got it.

"Do y'all want me to explain how this is different from *Silicon Valley*?" I asked.

The head executive in the room shook her head.

"No. We get it," she replied.

She stood and the rest of the room followed. I stood and offered a handshake. She pulled me into a hug.

"Hey, don't sell this to anybody until you hear from us."

I agreed. (Obviously.)

The next day I received an email from BET to buy my series.

◆ ◆

I was pacing in Jason Crain's loft apartment on Peters Street in Atlanta when I received word from my lawyers that the deal closed. Jason's place was across from 2 Chainz's restaurant, Escobar, on the west side. We were a fifteen-minute walk from Morehouse's campus, watching *SportsCenter* at noon on a weekday—just as we'd done countless times a decade before as college kids. The only difference was that this time we were stuffing our faces with kale wraps from Slutty Vegan instead of 99-cent chicken nuggets and double bacon cheeseburgers from Wendy's, our favorite budget-friendly delicacy as twenty-year-olds.

Jason's place had high ceilings and concrete floors, low lighting and portraits of Black pioneers painted by Jason himself. The Obamas. Prince. Mike Tyson. The fridge was always full, the bathrooms were loaded with a wide variety of toiletries, the closets were stacked high with linen. The sprawling loft seemed way too well supplied to belong to an early thirties bachelor.

"When I was growing up, we never had any of the shit people needed at the house," Jason explained. "So I never want that to be an issue here."

Ding. A text rang into my phone from my (Black) entertainment lawyer. He'd earned his JD at Howard University School of Law, where my dad was now a professor.

"I think we're resolved on all the deal points. After you review, you can go ahead and sign," my lawyer's text read.

"Yo, can I get your laptop?" I asked Jason.

"Sure," he said, handing it over. "What's up?"

"We're about to sign the deal," I said. I couldn't believe it. "I'm selling my show."

I grabbed the computer, swiftly typing in my credentials to DocuSign the contract as if it were going to evaporate if I didn't move quickly enough. Jason's face broke into a big, earnest smile. Two years earlier he'd sold Partpic, the hardware recognition software company he cofounded with Jewel Burks, to Amazon. He knew the struggle of entrepreneurialism. He too had watched his savings dwindle as he built something he believed in. He knew the loneliness and the voices that came at night, some telling him he was moving in the right direction, others saying he was blowing his best years on a pipe dream.

He also knew I needed money.

He bumped my shoulder with his forearm, shaking me a little. I reviewed the contract, whispering the legal jargon to myself. Click, click, click. I entered the day's date.

"You excited?" he asked.

I had dreamed of this moment for over a year. I had gone "all in" on this show. And now it had a network home. I punched in my e-signature and sent the contract back to my lawyer and the network's business affairs team. The deal was done. I'd be paid within a couple weeks. I expected to feel euphoric. But I didn't.

I looked up at Jason. He knew how I really felt.

"I'm relieved," I said.

I bit down on my lower lip. Jason nodded.

"I'm relieved," I said again, this time to myself.

"Congrats. You're not broke anymore," Jason joked.

Relief washed over me. Not triumph. Not elation. Those feelings visited over the following weeks and months, but they never overwhelmed me the way relief did. I was grateful to Spike for believing in an unproven first-timer. I was grateful to BET for investing in a young, Black creator. But mostly, I was relieved. When we sold the show, I was close to the end of my money and the end of my hope.

I leaned back on Jason's black leather couch. I stared ahead at the moving images on the wall from Jason's projector. The room was silent except for the hum of the air conditioner. Jason is a big guy who kept that place cold. I was exhausted. After a few minutes, a new feeling flooded in to replace the relief. Shame.

Why was BET the only network willing to invest in me and

my show? Was I not good enough for the other networks? Was I making a *Black* show?

I was. That was clear. But was that somehow not good enough for the other networks with white audiences?

This new feeling confused me. BET made shows with millions of weekly viewers, like *Girlfriends*, *The Game*, and *Being Mary Jane*. My goal was to reach millions of Black people with my show. I wanted to honestly portray the struggle of Black entrepreneurialism. There was no more immediate path to a high volume of Black viewers than this network.

But I felt rejected. The passes from other networks reminded me of feeling *othered* in classrooms, less than *Googly* at Google, alone and isolated in white worlds. The fact that those networks had turned me down even with Spike's partnership made it sting worse. Why didn't they revere Spike the way I did? And their insinuations that my show would be some kind of knockoff version of *Silicon Valley* infuriated me.

I went to visit my friend Elaine Welteroth at her *Teen Vogue* office, dozens of stories high in the One World Trade Center building where Condé Nast is headquartered. Her office was cluttered with vision boards, magazine clippings, and boxes upon boxes of hair and skin products sent by companies hoping for her endorsement. Elaine had just been promoted to editor in chief of the young woman's fashion, beauty, and entertainment magazine, and she was turning it into much more than that—a place of political activism and empowerment, especially for young women of color. Elaine's days were packed with meetings, so I met her there around 8 p.m. She was sitting behind her desk typing the last edits to her cover story. Her laptop sat atop scrawled-up magazine copy. A master multitasker, she alternated her focus between her laptop and my face. I was staring out her giant office windows over the lit-up Manhattan skyline toward the Statue of Liberty.

I vented to Elaine about the rejection I felt from the networks. I told her it was drowning out the excitement I wanted to feel for selling my show. I told her I was going to write an op-ed piece for a magazine explaining how proud I was to have the opportunity to work with BET. I was going to play defiance instead of disappointment, and share with everyone how lucky I felt to have this historic network behind me. She let me finish. Then she stopped typing to examine me over wide gold-rimmed glasses. She raised an eyebrow.

"Why not just tell the truth?" she asked. "Why not write something honest about feeling like a castoff because you're Black selling a Black product? You could focus the op-ed on being vulnerable instead of defensive. You could say you're grateful BET exists to take chances on underrepresented writers like you."

I chewed on her suggestion on the A train back to Brooklyn. A lesson found me. What I looked at as the *back door* to the industry was the *Black door*. And the Black door had been great to me all my life.

My opportunities had always come from people who looked like me. White people rarely cosigned me. It was Black people who had somehow seen me and pulled me through a door or pushed my résumé to the top of a stack. Straight up Black nepotism was my aid. Spike was my industry stamp. My manager was Black. My agent was Black. Jason referred me to Google. My mentors at the company, Ed and LaFawn Bailey, were a Black power couple. When I left Google in search of a startup job, another close Black friend from Morehouse made the connection that led me to Dev Bootcamp. I went to Morehouse in the first place because one of the deans saw something in me and gave me a full ride.

Each one of these people helped squeeze me into new spaces where I wouldn't have gotten on my own or waiting on white acceptance. I had to walk through the Black door to get into the building. The Black door is Black Magic.

ELAINE WELTEROTH

"And my best friend responds jokingly, 'What do I look like, your nigger?'"

Elaine is a *New York Times* bestselling author, award-winning journalist, screenwriter, producer, and *Project Runway* host. She began her career at *Ebony*, and has held senior roles at *Glamour* and *Teen Vogue*. In 2017, Elaine was named editor in chief of *Teen Vogue*, where she became the second Black person in Condé Nast's history to hold such a title. In 2018, she became one of the celebrity judges of Bravo's revamped *Project Runway*. Elaine has appeared on ABC's hit show *Black-ish* and has written for the show's spinoff *Grown-ish*. She is also an advocate for young women and Black and brown people from underserved backgrounds. She grew up in Newark, California, and earned her BA in Mass Communications, Media Studies and Journalism at Sacramento State.

Elaine is talented and confident. I met her when she began dating one of my best friends from college, who she has since married. Early in our friendship Elaine earned the title of editor in chief at *Teen Vogue* and we had frequent conversations about the challenges of earning and then maintaining high responsibility leadership roles as a Black person. But when I sat down to interview her for this book—first on the fifteenth floor of an old Fort Greene high-rise, then in an Uber on the way back from a film premiere where she moderated a conversation between the film's producer and director—I learned that as a child she'd felt squeezed between Black and white spaces.

Elaine is biracial. Her mother is Black and her father is

white. I was surprised by how much time and energy she has spent trying to prove herself to Black people *and* white people. As a mixed race child, she felt the need to prove she was loyal to the Black kids around her. As a young professional breaking into the beauty industry at *Ebony*, she felt she had to prove the iconic Black magazine's worth to white industry peers. The Elaine I know seems so different from the one who felt like "discount clothes" in the early stages of her career.

Elaine explained that having to defend and navigate her racial identity made her a more effective and empathetic communicator. She felt like she had to be the "bridge in the divide" between races, which made her patient with people's ignorance, fears, and misunderstandings. Elaine believes those skills allow her to create, lead, and connect people as a professional. Elaine believes that Black Magic is real, a gift from our ancestors. Then how do we tap into our Black Magic? She thinks we draw it from the subconscious.

Chad: What does the term "racial duality" evoke for you?

Elaine: I think of code-switching and assimilation. I think of the experience of being Black in corporate America. I think of being mixed race in America and being the bridge in the divide between races. I think of being "too Black" to fit into white spaces and "too white" for Black spaces. I think of the ways in which Black culture asks if you are "Black enough" when you are socialized in a white world. For me, being mixed race added a layer of "light skin privilege," which has historically been used to divide us as a community. Especially in my early years, I found myself contending with the "Am I Black enough?" question in certain spaces.

Chad: Who asks you to answer that question?

Elaine: I don't confront that question today, but growing up I felt that tension in certain Black social environments, whether it was at church or at the "Black table" at school. It was not an explicit question someone asked me, but it was in the subtext of many of the interactions I had with Black people, and there was a certain degree of code switching going on. I've had to code switch to fit into both worlds. Growing up, I was not accepted in groups of Black girls and I didn't feel particularly safe there.

Chad: Physically safe?

Elaine: I didn't always feel particularly welcome. At that point, I generally felt more psychologically safe around white girls because my best friends that I grew up with were mostly white. They were my sisters, and race had never been an issue—until it happens. And then it can never unhappen.

Chad: When did it happen?

Elaine: One night we were having a sleepover at one of my best friend's houses. Her parents came from a much more conservative part of the country. We were all talking in her bedroom, and then there was this moment where her friend says to her, "Can you please go get me some water from the kitchen?"

And my best friend responds jokingly, "What do I look like? Your nigger?"

It was one of those moments where your whole world stops. Everyone in the room stopped breathing. And it occured to me that I don't know if they would have skipped a beat if I wasn't there. I became "Black" in that moment. I never felt Black around them because they never made me feel Black. I never felt other until that moment.

I was in seventh or eighth grade, and it just felt like somebody knocked the wind out of me; somebody I really loved. She didn't mean to, but she did. It was like this curtain was pulled back and I saw something I never thought existed in my world. Immediately, just as soon as the words came out of her mouth, she just started crying. And everyone looked at me. I just felt like I wanted to disappear.

Chad: And what was the fallout?

Elaine: I don't really remember how the rest of the night progressed. You kind of black it out. Maybe because it was some form of trauma. I think she left the room, and then it was sort of on me to determine "How do I react to this?" As far as I can recall, we never talked about it again. To this day, I don't think we've ever really talked about it.

Chad: You're still friends?

Elaine: I was the maid of honor at her wedding. I helped her write her vows.

Chad: Was that incident when you realized you were Black?

Elaine: My parents were intentional about making sure I owned my Blackness. They made sure [my brother and I] knew we were Black and that we knew our history and our culture. So even though we grew up in a white neighborhood, my mom was insistent on us going to a Black church. That was part of our culture. That was very important for us. She put us in the kids' gospel choir at church. She told me that before we were born my parents talked about the fact that they were going to be raising Black kids; that we would identify as Black. They knew that regardless of our genetics, the world was going to see us as Black. That was important for us to understand from an early age.

My very first memory in life is rooted in racial duality. I was around three years old at a predominantly-white preschool. We were given a stack of magazines as part of an assignment to make a family collage. As I flipped through the pages, I didn't see anyone that looked like me or my family. So, I remember cutting out pictures of white people. The teacher caught on and came to encourage me to cut out the only Black girl she could find in one of the magazines. I remember her gently saying, "Oh, she's so pretty! What about her? She looks like you! She has such pretty hair like you. . . ."

And I—ignored her. I acted like she wasn't even talking to me. I completely iced her because I wanted to just be like everyone else so badly. I remember feeling embarrassed after a while because she started talking to the other teacher about it but I didn't even want to acknowledge them because then I'd have to face my own difference. So, I kept pasting white people onto my family collage. That night when I came home, my mom sat me and my brother down with the collage out in front of us and she said, "We have to talk about this." I could tell I did something wrong from the tone of her voice. I knew what she was going to tell me. But I didn't want to face it. She pulled out *Ebony* and *Essence* magazines and told us that we were going to redo this little preschool assignment together as a family. My mom made me take off the white people from my collage and replace them with Black people. Only my dad's picture could stay because he was already white [laughs].

I have another memory from childhood deeply rooted in racial duality. I think I was turning ten and I really wanted a ballerina doll that I'd seen on TV commercials. I was harassing my mom about it. I *really* wanted it. She waited in a long line and went through so much to get the doll for me. My birthday comes and all my friends are there. I opened up her gift and it was the Black version of the doll. I guess it was obvious from my body language that I didn't want it.

My mom said, "Girl, you've been harassing me about this doll. I went through hell and high water to get it for you. What is the problem?"

"I wanted the other one," I said.

"What other one?" she asked me. She had to probe me, but I eventually confessed that I wanted the one from the commercial. The blonde one. I knew even then that maybe I wasn't supposed to want the white doll, but I did because of the way it was presented to me. But my mom—once again—intentionally redirected me to confront and embrace my Blackness by never buying me white dolls. Still, I felt shame for not being white and shame for the part of me that wanted to be white.

Chad: When have you most recently felt that same way?

Elaine: My relationship to my race has changed so much. I think my shame has turned to pride. Genuinely. That sounds cheesy, but it really has. It wasn't overnight. I feel my Blackness in my career right now in ways that are holding me back, and the only shame I feel about it is "shame on them." There is a certain unapologetic defiance that I feel about the ways that I stand out now.

Chad: What created the transformation between the shame that you felt then to the pride you feel today?

Elaine: Validation from my own community. Which came, over time, through my work.

But I also encountered the shame again early on in my career when I realized Black magazines aren't regarded as highly as white magazines. I thought, *Oh, I'm on the wrong side of this.* I came in really hot, full of dreams. Really excited about breaking into this industry that was so elusive to me. I was excited about [New York] City and starting out at *Ebony* magazine. I get there, and on day one I cried in the bathroom. I realized just how underresourced the magazine was and the unique challenges that come along with working in Black media. There is this perception in the industry that the editors that work there are second-tier. There was this latent fear that I would have a harder time being taken seriously if and when I desired to "crossover" to a mainstream magazine. I started to feel embarrassed that I worked there. I had to deal with the "white is right" thing all over again. So I immediately decided from day one that to operate among the best of the best, I had to dream a bigger dream. That dream became working at Condé Nast, because it was considered the most prestigious publishing house—where "the best of the best" work. Particularly because that's where *Vogue* is published. I remember thinking, "I gotta get myself there."

It took a long time because there's a caste system in fashion media. *Ebony* magazine was at the lowest rung. It wasn't chic or regarded highly by fashion houses. The fight of having to prove myself began there; proving that I deserved to be there; proving that we *should* be invited to Fashion Week and that we *should* be backstage. I was the underdog. But even as I was fighting for *Ebony* externally, there were times internally when I was made to feel that I wasn't necessarily a "culture fit" at *Ebony*. It came with some of the "crabs in the barrel" mentality that I had experienced at the proverbial "Black table" in high school. At times I felt like I couldn't win either way.

Then, when I went to these fancy beauty appointments with all the white girls from the white magazines, I felt like discount clothes [laughs]. There was this constant negotiation of your value in that world and what defined your worth. In my interview process with white magazines, I felt like hiring managers from these titles didn't know what to do with me. I know that I interview well. I know that I present well. But it felt like they just couldn't quite pull the trigger in a way that I don't think they would admit to.

Chad: What did you feel like when you left *Ebony* magazine?

Elaine: Vindicated. It felt like evidence that you can be Black and proud and start your career at *Ebony* and also bring those values to white media. But on some level, crossing over was also about credibility and validation. Once I got to *Glamour*, one thing I never did, that I could have done, was wipe my résumé. I've seen people leave a place they're not proud of and never mention it again once they make it to a place that's perceived as more prestigious. I never, ever did that. *Ebony* was such a formative time for me, personally and professionally. It formed the bedrock of my career. It helped shape who I am as a professional. *Ebony* is the only reason I'm here. Black media validated me and gave me opportunity before anyone else; it is so important that we continue to validate Black media. I want my work to further validate pride in Blackness and Black culture. We're in a day and age—what the film *Get Out* brilliantly alluded to—where people want to borrow Black culture and appropriate it when it's convenient, when they can profit from it. But Blackness still isn't valued.

Chad: How was your experience different when you crossed over to *Glamour* and *Teen Vogue*?

Elaine: After *Ebony*, I went to *Glamour* and then *Teen Vogue* where being heralded as the first Black beauty director at Condé Nast helped put into context what my particular seat at the table could mean. I was in a unique and unprecedented position. The responsibility that comes with that, the weight of that, hit me and it felt powerful. Some of my value add was that I am Black and I could bring a perspective that no one else there had and I could reach an audience there that no one else could. I could change the game there like no one else had.

I was able to embrace my Blackness in a way that felt uniquely rewarding. My first story was about my natural hair journey—embracing it. Telling the story of how growing up, I equated good hair with straight hair, and I never felt pretty for special occasions unless my hair was straight. How wrong I had it! That was just the beginning of ushering in a different kind of cultural conversation and social consciousness to the magazine. That period of awakening allowed me to bring more of myself to work. And to better align my work with my authentic self.

Chad: When have you intentionally evoked whiteness? And how do you do it, and what has it afforded you?

Elaine: You mean code-switch?

Chad: Sure, if that's the vehicle.

Elaine: I don't think that's fair to say. Black people, like everyone, possess multitudes. I don't think it's fair to say "When were you being white?" "When were you being Black?" I get your question, but I think it's kind of problematic.

I am well spoken. Does that mean I'm trying to be white? I can also flex another muscle that's a little more street. What makes that Black? I don't think I've ever tried to be white. I'm aware that colorism is a real thing and I'm aware that to folks who are unaware of their bias that I may seem somewhat "less intimidating" because of my skin color and the way I look and the way I express myself because of the ways in which I was institutionally socialized in white spaces.

Chad: Do you wield that?

Elaine: Wield it? I am who I am. It's not like I'm trying to use aspects of my identity to my advantage. But I am conscious of the ways in which I can be a bridge in the divide. Some aspects of my identity might make it easier to open doors. But the other parts of my identity will change the nature of the game once I'm on the other side of it and keep the door open for people who look like me as well as people who don't look like me but have a really valuable outside perspective to share.

Chad: When do you evoke Blackness and what does it do for you?

Elaine: I'm just unapologetically Black.

Chad: What does unapologetic Blackness look like?

Elaine: It looks like being free enough to communicate however I am feeling in that moment. That might include using colloquial terms and being free enough to express myself without feeling the pressure to conform to some sort of conventional standard of what a professional corporate leader or executive is supposed to look like or sound like. It's a power move when I decide to switch into being comfortable enough to be myself.

Chad: So when do you decide not to do that? Can you give an example?

Elaine: When I feel like it won't be received well or won't reflect well on us. Certain formal settings.

Chad: So you are in those moments suppressing your Blackness?

Elaine: Not suppressing it, but I might express it in a different way. I will still be the person who will talk about diversity and inclusion unapologetically, and I can speak intelligently about Blackness. But I might be more conscious of what they're expecting of a Black stereotype and I don't want to deliver that. I want to break that mold. This is interesting, because I don't ever think about it this deeply.

Chad: Have you ever intentionally evoked more Blackness for any reason?

Elaine: Hmm. Maybe around my Black friends in college, I'd speak a certain way. It goes back to that childhood trauma and judgment. I just didn't want them to think I thought I was better than them. I might have spoken more like them in their presence sometimes just because I wanted them to feel comfortable with me. I think that's a really natural, normal thing to do. I don't think it's about Black and white as much as it's about wanting people to feel comfortable and connected to you. It's an empathetic thing.

Chad: How have you engaged with your father's whiteness?

Elaine: I don't know that I ever have. I've never talked to him about being white—except for the obvious jokes around his lack of rhythm [laughs]. Me being biracial is so deeply a part of who I am. Whether other people are aware of it or not, I'm aware that I am able to navigate certain rooms, certain groups, more seamlessly, because I can really relate with white people on a level that I think has something to do with being half-white and being socialized around white people for most of my life.

I have had to educate white folks about Black people and Black culture. And I suppose I have this weird empathy for them and this weird empathy for their lack of exposure—which we all have to some extent. People of color often bear the brunt of their ignorance and carry that extra weight. We see white privilege every single day, and we haven't always been able to call it out, so we have learned to navigate around it.

Chad: What are some ways that you can relate to whiteness?

Elaine: I relate in having good intentions but not quite getting it right. Their desire to celebrate Blackness but expressing it in a cringey way. Wanting to make people feel comfortable and overshooting. Their naivete and their ignorance. I excuse it because I grew up with it. My dad does things that are cringey sometimes and I think, *Oh my God, don't do that around Black people, okay?*

When I was in college [at Sacramento State] I really dealt with this negotiation of race in the most consistent way. My college was very segregated and there was always this racial divide in terms of "who am I gonna' sit with?" "Who am I gonna party with?" I was placed in my dorm room with a white girl and we fell in friend love with each other. She became one of my best friends. There were these other white girls down the hall who became our good friends as well and that quickly became my core group. But I felt skittish about being classified as that token Black girl who hangs out with the white people. I really felt that tension if there was a Black person around and I was with white people. I felt like I had to choose. It felt like a decision I was conscious of almost all the time. I started to become intentional about making Black girlfriends—I really wanted that because I never had it. I wanted to nurture those new friendships, which felt like an instant sisterhood, but I could feel a certain resistance on their part, of not wanting to be around white people.

I felt like a bridge between worlds when I brought my white friends and Black friends together and we all went to my first college house party. My new white girlfriends suggested the party. And we didn't make it up the driveway before I was called a nigger. This drunk white guy bumped into me and then yelled in my face, "*Watch where you're going, you fucking nigger.*"

Again, it's that moment when you're taken almost outside of yourself. While this was happening, my white girlfriends were so drunk they were peeing on the same front lawn I was standing on just a few feet away while I got called a nigger. They didn't even hear it. When I told them, they were shocked and appalled but they could only empathize so much. They felt guilty for bringing me there, but ultimately, in a way, it was this white guilt, that I had to sort of coddle whereas my Black friends created a safe space. They said, "See, this is why we don't fuck with these parties."

But then I remember going to Georgia for the first time in the summer to visit my mom's side of the family. We spent all summer there. I was finally feeling like I was having fun, out of my shell. I was jumping on a trampoline with my cousin Mark, who is Black, and two Black girls drove by on bicycles and yelled, "Mark's hanging out with the white girl! Why are you hanging out with that white girl?" It was the same jarring feeling. It sent me out of my skin. I was wearing braids, think-ing *How the fuck am I white? What? It feels like a punch in the chest. I just felt so "other."*

So, I don't know. Growing up, I just felt like a pinball in a pinball machine.

Chad: How have you applied what you've learned from your racial suffering?

Elaine: Empathy. I think that one of the greatest strengths we have as minorities is empathy. Struggle teaches us empathy. Discrimination teaches us empathy.

Chad: How is it useful?

Elaine: Right now, what this world needs, to heal itself, is em-pathy. Understanding another person's perspective and being willing to allow empathy to be the bridge in the divide—that's a superpower. It's one that Black people possess uniquely. We're the most creative people on the planet in part because of our racial struggles. That's the result of oppression. When we're suppressed, our creativity becomes a necessary form of expression for our humanity; to feel our humanity, to express our humanity. Because of the experience of oppression in this country, our art is among the most potent in the world. The richest forms of expression come from the African diaspora. The most powerful pieces of cinema, music, dance, writing, over the last year, are authored by Black people.

I have been among the artists of this generation whose art has been elevated at a time such as this when we are finally being exalted. I think that we are living through an age where we are seeing this reclamation of our culture. We no longer are allowing other groups to co-opt our culture because of the historical erasure of Black art and the credit, the authorship, of which we have been stripped. Because of generations of culture-vulturing, we've hit this point, a deafening crescendo in terms of lack of representation. We're also among the loudest voices on social media, and the rise of social media has given us a platform to say, "Hey, we're here too and we matter. Black Lives Matter. Black Art Matters. Black Culture Matters."

There has been this collective snatch back of what is ours and we're creating on a fucking prolific scale. Look at the Black art that's come out recently. From Barry Jenkins's *Moonlight* to Solange's *A Seat at the Table* to Ava DuVernay's *13th* to Ta-Nehisi Coates's *Between the World and Me* to Jordan Peele's *Get Out*. All of that is a result of generations of oppression.

Chad: Do you believe in Black Magic? Do you think it's real?

Elaine: Yes. 100 percent. 100 percent.

Chad: Do you think you have to believe it's real to access it?

Elaine: No. It's a part of who we are. It's involuntary. It's in the way we move. It's in the way we express ourselves. It's in our bloodline. You don't necessarily have to be conscious of it to access it. It's a gift from our ancestors.

The N-Word

My friend Sterling, a Black man, worked as an analyst at JP-Morgan in his first year out of college. His colleagues were mostly white kids from Ivy League schools who worked long days, some powered by Adderall and cocaine, all for the opportunity to later move into higher power/stress/salary Wall Street jobs. Sterling's free time was rare. On Friday nights, he would meet me at the bars on the Lower East Side around 2 a.m., still in his suit.

Once, I was at Piano's, a popular bar downtown, when Sterling came ambling in at 1:45 a.m. By the time he found our crew on the second floor, he was already halfway through his second Maker's neat. It usually took him two or three drinks to settle down after leaving his desk, where he sat alert for up to twenty hours a day thanks to caffeine and other drugs.

"Wattup fool?" he said when he saw me. He was still gnawing at nothing in his mouth while the uppers wore off.

"Bruh, are you good?" I said. "You look T'd."

I reminded him of something he already knew. His suit was impressive, but his dilated pupils and baggy, bloodshot eyes conveyed anxiety, not confidence. He was sleep-deprived, and skittish.

"Dude, I've been having the weirdest dream," he began. "Over and over. I can't sleep. Every night I have this nightmare that Colin . . . Colin, the white dude at my desk who went to UVA . . ." He was always complaining about the people at his desk.

"So I keep having this dream that we're all sitting there at our desks and our boss comes over to ask us if we're done with something. Then me and Colin get into it," he said.

Sterling was staring really hard at the floor. Occasionally, he'd look up at me and touch his chest for emphasis.

"And Colin's like yo, you said you were on it. Where is it? And he keeps just like pressing me on it, pressing me on it. Now my boss is looking at us. And other people are starting to circle around us. And it's just like me and Colin in the middle of all these white people just watching us in this argument. And I'm like, dude, Colin, it's chill. I'm on top of it. And Colin stands up and he goes, 'It's not fucking chill, Nigger!'"

Sterling's movements get wilder. I pat his back to calm him down. People are starting to watch us, like they watched *him* in the dream.

"You ever had that dream?" he asked me.

"Not that one exactly. But I know Ray and Pop have had something similar," I reassured him. Ray and Pop were our friends who were also Black, working similar hours, doing similar drugs to stay awake, at Goldman Sachs. Sterling took a long swig of his drink.

"So what do you do in the dream?" I asked.

"It's different every time," he said. "I think it depends on how my coworkers react. In one they all start laughing and I jump out the window. In another someone grabs me from behind and I attack Colin, but they all gang up on me and pin me down. Then I wake up. One time, when he said the word 'Nigger,' it spilled out of his mouth into soup at his feet.

I'm terrified, dude. I'm terrified that it's gonna happen because I keep thinking about it. Like I'm gonna make it happen by thinking about it so much. Colin's never said anything like that to me. He does the normal douche bag microaggression shit but nothing even close to an attack. It's scaring me, man."

Sterling and I just stood there under the music holding our drinks. I understood exactly where he was coming from. My friends had shared similar nightmares connecting their feelings of isolation to the intense performance pressure they shouldered at big investment banks. Looking back, I would suggest Sterling talk to someone, maybe enter therapy, to deal with such strong and scary feelings. But I didn't know what to say, then. So I just stood with him for a moment, nodding. Our friend Kaylin, an Asian woman in her early twenties, emerged with another round of drinks.

"Hey, what are you guys talking about?" she asked.

"We're just chillin'," Sterling replied. "Yo, I love this song!"

◆ ◆

I empathize with Sterling's fear of the n-word encroaching on his life unexpectedly. The n-word is a constant in my life in all its permutations. Nigga. Nigger. Negro.

I use the n-word at *least* daily and sometimes more, depending on who I'm with and what kind of music I'm listening to. My parents never let me use the word in our house growing up. I remember being shocked when a friend's mom called him a "trifling nigga" for leaving the garage door open overnight. My dad said that people who used the word lacked a robust vocabulary. He felt the same way about the use of profanity.

"People use curse words when they're not quick enough to

describe a concept or feeling with precision," he said. But still, I'd often hear him in his home office with the doors closed blasting Tupac and MC Hammer. "Rap is different," he said. "The best rappers are geniuses. They're experts of language."

I started saying nigga at Morehouse as a familial term. Today, I often hear the word coming from the mouths of my close friends using it to disarm me, telling me that we're in a safe space where we can discuss life without pretension. But we acknowledge the word's horrific history and connotations. We know the word was sometimes the last phrase our ancestors heard uttered as they were lynched. We don't mean to evoke the scary or violent connotations. My friends and I use the word as a way to say I see you, I love you, and I feel what you're going through.

But the n-word ended my friendship with a white guy instantly a few years ago. Brett was curious and wry and down to earth. He was a native New Yorker and a woke bro; the kind of white guy who always knows the trending social justice hashtags and asks people their pronouns before engaging. We became friends working together at the tech startup. We started hanging out after work too. He invited me to parties with his rich friends from wealthy neighborhoods in New Jersey that I'd never heard of much less visited until then. There were bonfires.

I often tokened at Brett's parties. By *tokened* I mean, I showed up as one of only a couple Black attendees and played up my *Blackness* to have a place in the group. I'd make punchy jokes about how the white people at the party didn't know the words to the rap songs they played, or about how I was the only one getting carded by the bouncers at the bars. These experiences were actually humiliating. I felt like a sellout making fun of race to feel comfortable, but the folks at the parties laughed when I did. I was peacocking racially. I'm not proud of that behavior.

I was tokening at a party with Brett the night he blew up our friendship. We were at a backyard Brooklyn shindig with a piñata. Maybe thirty white people in their mid-twenties were in attendance wearing nineties basketball jerseys and crocs and vintage TLC shirts. I stood with Brett and his friend Mikey. We small talked, holding our beers at stiff, ninety-degree angles. Future played in the background. We were prattling about hip-hop, which surely one of them had brought up. I steer clear of hip-hop and sports as discussion topics with white people when there is booze involved, because of the racial landmines around those mainly Black professions. I feel triggered when they use coded language to describe our athletes in dehumanizing ways.

"LeBron James is a natural talent, freak of nature."

"Zion Williamson is an absolute manchild. He won the genetic lottery. The Pelicans should *never* trade that one. He's a beast. Ah, and he's so handsome. That bright smile with those shining white teeth." No, thank you.

But on this night, none of my subtle subject changes held up. I was reasonably safe, I thought, because I was with Brett, a woke bro.

Then Brett made the Face. THAT FACE. The one that my five-year-old buddy Eric made before he said Black people looked like poop in preschool. The Face white people make when they're about to say something they know they shouldn't but just can't help themselves. The provocateur face, emboldened by the shield of their whiteness. The Joe Rogan face. The Will Cain face. The Colin Cowherd face. Before I could distract him, Brett went for it.

"Honestly though, 'Niggas in Paris' was the best song of the decade."

Mikey stared at the ground. Hearing *the word* made my stomach drop. I thought through a billion fight-or-flight calculations in a moment. I eyed the exits. There was one at the front of the apartment complex, another through the back gate of the yard. I noticed a Black woman I'd met a few times before, standing with her back against the gate, holding a glass of wine, over-laughing at the two tall white guys with shaggy beards doing impressions beside her. If my response incited an argument, or worse, would I be putting her at risk too?

I thought about just walking away. I could make up an excuse about why I had to leave the party. I didn't want to face the humiliation I felt, but if I swallowed this moment down, I would never feel truly comfortable around Brett again. I could never be vulnerable, I could never relax my defenses. And I'd have to pretend that everything was normal. That would be unbearable. The thought gave me a self-righteous kick of courage.

"You shouldn't say that, dude," I announced. I had my father's steely tone. I watched Brett's movements carefully. How would he respond? His friend nodded in deference to me. He gave me the bare minimum in agreement. It was Brett who pushed back.

"It's the title of the song," Brett started. "What? How am I supposed to reference the song? *They* named it that."

He was obviously trying to be provocative, because otherwise how would he even know what I was reacting to?

"You guys need anything?" Mikey asked before awkwardly bowing out of the conversation to grab another beer. We ignored him.

"What's the problem? It's part of the song!" Brett questioned. He was incredulous.

"Yeah, I just don't like when you say it. It's not for you to say," I replied.

This is the problem with a question like the one Brett asked me. *Why can't he say the n-word if it's in the title of a popular rap song?* How was I supposed to answer that? Should I start with a history of slavery and the Middle Passage and work my way to this moment? Where do I even begin? How could I isolate the specific reason why he couldn't use the word? How could I explain that his use of it then had already dented our friendship and that it was all downhill as long as he resisted?

I didn't have words to articulate my feelings so I just said the truth. "*I just don't like it.*"

"Dude, it's not like I'm calling *you* the n-word," he insisted. "It's just a song. It doesn't even mean anything in this context. Why is it such a big deal?"

He was making it worse. The word meant *everything* in that context. The song was called "Niggas in Paris." It was an ode to defiance; Jay-Z and Kanye West, descendants of Black slaves turned billionaires, celebrating bloodlines that survived racial genocide. The word meant *everything*. (This was before Kanye became a Donald Trump disciple.)

Brett wanted me to defend my case. He wanted me to *explain* to him why he couldn't use the n-word. And as I thought about it, the truth was that he could use the word as he pleased. Brett was a chess player. He wanted me to debate semantics. It dawned on me that if my discomfort wasn't enough for him to stop using the word, then there was nothing I was going to explain to him with beers in hand that would make him walk off his position.

I eyed the back gate again. I left without another word. He and I never spoke again. I learned over the course of many Eric and Brett "friendships" that I was unwilling to uphold a friendship with someone who couldn't sacrifice a hurtful word for my dignity.

I estimated that Brett's indignation at the *injustice* of not being allowed to use the n-word was just the tip of the iceberg. I figured there must be other problematic racial stances under his waterline that would reveal themselves. I feared for my self-esteem. Was I guessing? Yes. I was using past *friendships* that showed *insensitive* warning signs and microaggressions early on, then eventually devolved into full-on attacks, verbal and physical. There was a kid in sixth grade who clung to me as a best friend for weeks then called me a nigger during a two-hand touch football game because I pushed him too hard. Or the twenty-seven-year-old colleague from Boston who presented as a friend for months, then had too many whiskeys one night and locked us in a bar bathroom at a work happy hour. He commanded me to "stop being a little Black pussy and hit him in the face." I refused. I didn't want to be arrested that night. I slipped out the back of the restroom. When I saw him the following Monday at work, he had forgotten the incident—or pretended he had. I also pretended to have forgotten the incident to avoid any interactions with Human Resources at our company.

If it sounds dramatic for me to abandon a friendship because a guy said the n-word, let me explain that it wasn't dramatic at all. The weight of the offense doesn't really matter here. Walking away felt easy. I didn't lose sleep. By that point, I had already learned the signs of a racially toxic friendship and I was ready to slam the eject button if I saw one of those signs.

SHELLEY STEWART

"In many environments, there's a scarce number of Black folks. Which comes with its own set of challenges. But, on the other hand, if I'm just honest, there's also this soft bigotry of low expectations. Once you realize it, you can actually turn it to your advantage."

Shelley Stewart III is a partner at McKinsey & Company—making him one of the 1 percent of partners in McKinsey North America who are Black. He was formerly a founding partner at the Dreadnought Group, an investment management firm where he led portfolio management. Shelley began his career as an analyst working in JPMorgan's investment bank focused on fixed income securities. Shelley earned his MBA at Columbia University and his BA in Economics at Boston College.

Shelley and I spoke about how his confidence positively affected his performance, and how other people with the same potential underperformed because they lack that confidence. But what really struck me was this: Shelley was honest about the disadvantages that come with being Black in a corporation, but he also pointed out the advantages. For example, Shelley said that Black people stand out in a corporation just for being Black—that makes us noteworthy to our colleagues, which gives us opportunities to connect with them and build trust. From there, Shelley believes, we have a responsibility to be open to those relationships and use them with a give-and-take attitude. Some might call this networking opportunism, but I appreciate Shelley's approach. There are enough forces working against us. We shouldn't feel shame for using our identities to build relationships when it suits us.

Shelley gave another powerful example of this kind of reframing when we spoke. He believes that Black people can make an asset of the low expectations levied on us by managers and higher-ups. He calls this the "soft bigotry of low expectations," which can slow us down when it means bosses give us fewer responsibilities with lower upside. But we can also make a name for ourselves quickly as high achievers by overdelivering on easy win projects, and shattering, as Shelley said, those low expectations. Shelley's vision for opportunity in imperfect circumstances is his Black Magic.

———

Shelley: I was very fortunate to grow up in a household where both parents were college educated. Both of my parents were first-generation college educated, both went on to get master's degrees, and so education was always front and center in my household.

My mom worked for the state of Connecticut and had a competitive job and managed people. I got to see that influence. And I got to watch my father's career start out from an entry-level job at a manufacturing company rising to be an executive. So, I actually got to see the full journey going up the income ladder in real time. I feel very fortunate to have seen that whole journey and to have been apprenticed to be a professional person and to have a certain level of confidence. I think that is critical to my success thus far.

Chad: You talked about jumping on an entrepreneurial track at one point in your professional career and now you're a partner at McKinsey & Company. How have you been able to apply lessons you learned growing up as a young Black man to those environments?

Shelley: That's a great question with a complicated answer. Two primary things come to mind. Somewhere along the way I picked up that there's a tremendous amount of disadvantage with being Black. There is also, depending on the environment you're in, this currency. You know? In many environments, there's a scarce number of Black folks. Which comes with its own set of challenges. But, on the other hand, if I'm just honest, there's also this soft bigotry of low expectations. Once you realize it, you can actually turn it to your advantage.

So consistently, whether it was at JPMorgan or my entrepreneurial venture or McKinsey, I think coming in and quickly shattering low expectations got me recognized. And then you have to continue to deliver and even over-deliver. I spend 70 percent of my non-client time at McKinsey trying to get more Black folks in the door. But I also recognize that in the near term, the scarcity may be a valuable commodity. Some of that is because companies know that they need to feed into diversity for shareholder optics or PR. Some of it is because, again, you need to vastly shatter their expectations, which causes you to rise in stock kind of quickly, relative to some of your peers. You can seize disadvantage and turn it into an opportunity if your perspective is such.

The caveat, which is the second point, is that I also had the benefit of having tremendous self-confidence. I believed that I should be in all the places that I was. That was a function of having strong role models. In my case, it was my parents and my grandfather. My grandfather never wanted to go to college, but he was still a tremendously strong role model. He was a labor leader and he worked the shop floor and had his own business after that. So I had people to look up to, so when I went to these places, I felt confident. That gave me the wind at my back to take advantage of some of the scarcity.

Chad: What about young Black people who aren't born with those types of role models? What advice do you give people who need mentors to show them the way in their careers?

Shelley: There are a couple of things that are important for young people looking for mentors or to build relationships. One is that you have to recognize that you have something in common with everyone. If you take a narrow view of what you have in common with people, you fall into a trap. You end up saying "I'm an only, I'm very different, I'm a young Black kid, I like this kind of music, I'm into this kind of fashion." And you have a very narrow view. You fall into this trap of thinking, "I have nothing in common with this twenty-seven-year-old Asian woman or this fifty-five-year-old white man."

When I was at JPMorgan, the ten people on my desk ranged from a sixty-five-year-old white guy to a twenty-four-year-old Asian woman and everything in between. This wasn't deliberate, but I found something in common with every single one of those people. And what that did was it brought in the potential pool of people who might decide to mentor and sponsor me. It's an important lesson if you come to McKinsey as a young Black person, I'm going to proactively seek you out. I'm super-passionate about that. One percent of the partners in McKinsey North America are Black. So there's not enough. What you have to do is build authentic connections with people, recognizing that common points come in a variety of shapes and forms. You have to be deliberate about that, and then you will have a high likelihood of getting mentored. That's the point.

The second thing is you have to think about how you can make the relationship mutually beneficial. Everyone is solving for something. What you need to find out is, how are you going to help elevate the performance of your mentor? Some people will mentor for the sake of mentoring. I think that's important—sponsoring for the sake of sponsoring. But, in the end, it's a much better relationship when it works both ways. If you go in with a mindset of "I want to be sponsored and mentored, *and* I'm going to also be deliberate about helping you be the best version of you, mentor," then I think you'll often find success.

I remember after business school when I reached out to Ursula Burns. At the time she was still CEO of Xerox. I just kind of cold-emailed her and said, "Hey, I would love for you to come in and speak to the Black students at Columbia." At first she said that Columbia had been asking a lot because she's an alum, and she's pretty busy, so she couldn't do it. I totally got it. It was a long shot. But I happened to write back and said, "Hey, by the way, Xerox is on campus trying to recruit, particularly looking for Black students. Let me know if you want me to keep an eye out for folks that would be good for management rotations." She wrote me back the next day and thanked me for the offer and said she'd love to come speak. That was a lesson for me that you need to make yourself a resource to people that can help you. They're much more likely to reciprocate if you do.

My third point is to ask *the* question. It's actually quite hard to ask the question, and you don't do it to random strangers. But if you start to build a relationship with someone in your place of work, you get to the point and trust your instincts and go out on a limb. Ask the question. "Will you look after me? Will you sponsor me?" It's okay to ask that question. I think people are afraid. The worst someone can say is no. But what you'll actually find is that people find it hard in those human moments to say no. If you spend some time investing in that person, it's more than likely they would love to sponsor you, they just may not have even thought about you that way until you explicitly ask. So, don't be afraid to ask the question.

Chad: I'm finding in these conversations a connection between Blackness and entrepreneurialism. My own theory is that in the face of lacking resources and opportunities, Black people had to be creative to find work and make money. What did you learn from being an entrepreneur early in your career?

Shelley: One of the misnomers that exists today—and I think you're right, some of it goes back to this trauma and lack of opportunities in our community—is the idea that you just gotta go do it. "I gotta put my head down and get it done and work." I think that is true in some instances, but I think if you look at entrepreneurship broadly and you look at pockets of success, my hypothesis is that the situations that really work out are the ones that are a little more rigged. Meaning, people either have an inside track on something, or they showed up with a full packed bag.

For us, if we're gonna go take an entrepreneurial risk, which I highly encourage, we need to make sure we understand and have a true value proposition for the endeavor. Either we have a unique skill innately or one that we've developed, or we have to put the team together to do it. But truly knowing your source of distinctiveness and your limitations is the most critical thing to increasing the likelihood of that endeavor being successful.

Chad: There must have been someone who grew up with nearly identical opportunities and circumstances to yours who never reached similar levels of success. Why would that happen?

Shelley: Unfortunately, I can cite far too many people in my life like that. The nexus of self-confidence and ambition is so important. I think some of my friends who grew up in similar situations did not have the self-confidence to aspire anymore. They set their sights far too low at the outset, and that became self-fulfilling. And I think, in many cases, it was a lack of self-confidence that led to lower ambition which led them to not strive for more.

QUINCY AVERY

"You gotta use the thing that others might use against you to benefit in other areas. You have to figure out what it is you're good at and what it is you can do. You have to figure out what it is that your Black skin might help you advance with."

Quincy is the world's top quarterback trainer. His clients include NFL MVP Patrick Mahomes, NFL Pro Bowler Deshaun Watson, NFL first-round draft picks Dwayne Haskins, EJ Manuel, and Johnny Manziel, as well as NFL starter Tyrod

Taylor and Ohio State Buckeyes star Justin Fields. As the son of an NFL coach, Quincy has spent thousands of hours in locker rooms and on football fields. Quincy earned his BA in Psychology at Morehouse College, where he played wide receiver on the football team.

In our conversation, Quincy spoke openly about his childhood, and the early years of his career when things weren't easy. When Quincy was growing up, his father struggled with drug addiction and once left Quincy alone in a hotel room for days. Quincy lived in his car for a few years after college while he worked for unlivable wages to jump-start his football training career. He built his business on his own, through unconventional means. Quincy chased down prospective clients on social media to build up his roster and show his expertise. He bet on himself by living broke for a few years to get his business going. He seemed never to mind that some of our peers were making faster money through more traditional jobs at tech companies and banks. Quincy was always relentlessly focused on the present moment and the things immediately under his control, which may have come from feeling so out of control as the son of a drug addict.

In the fifteen years I've known Quincy, I've never heard him complain about these experiences. Quincy looks at struggle and joy with the same twinkle in his eye. He sees both as necessary parts of building something that is his. And while we spoke about many topics, that's the message that stayed with me long after.

Quincy laughed through most of our conversation—and that's his usual demeanor. Quincy's joy is infectious—and he knows it. He uses it to his advantage. He says you have to carry a certain pizzazz to make your mark as a Black professional. That is Black Magic.

————————

Quincy: I am the owner of Quarterback Takeover. What we do is train the top quarterbacks across the country, whether they're NFL, college, high school, we train the elite quarterbacks. We train the most elite people at the most elite position in all of sports.

Chad: What lessons have you learned through your Black experience that have helped you succeed in your field?

Quincy: I think the number one lesson that I've probably learned is the art of perseverance. Not only persevering, but being willing to change your course, or change your sails along that course of perseverance. It's not just necessarily about working hard and staying on the path, but being able to adjust to different things and stay through it while you're trying to get to a certain destination. I think that's really the most important part in this whole journey. It's kinda what's allowed me to be successful.

Chad: Where did you learn perseverance?

Quincy: I grew up as a Black man. It's a unique perspective because I was middle-class, but I went to a school that was very, very diverse. Being the African-American kid, you have to learn how to shapeshift, almost. Like you gotta be a chameleon. You feel like you gotta be able to relate to all the Black kids and then at the same time you gotta gain the respect of the white kids. So, you've gotta be able to do both, especially in my occupation. If

I hadn't been able to do those things, then I wouldn't have been able to be great in both settings.

I work with almost all of the top Black NFL quarterbacks. That takes a certain level of charisma that you're gonna have to have as a Black man, but also I have to go into the same meetings with Fortune 500 companies in order to get sponsorships and things of that nature. I have to be able to play both sides of the fence. I have to be able to adapt to each situation. My experience growing up taught me how to be fluid.

Chad: How is your experience working with players and families of Black backgrounds different from the players and families that you engage with from other backgrounds?

Quincy: When dealing with African-American families, I think I understand the struggle they may be going through. I've just seen it. I've seen the single moms. I've seen the dads trying to do whatever they could to get their sons an advantage. I've seen the younger culture of Black parents. We see a lot of split households, where Dad is very involved, and they might not be together so he has to do whatever he can to be helpful in that role.

Dealing with Black families, I want to be more helpful, in a way, because I know how difficult it is to be a Black quarterback and to be successful. Most of sports is like a meritocracy, almost, so usually the best person gets the job. That's the case pretty much throughout sports. But, I think that the quarterback position is different. There are more hurdles you have to go through. So, the quarterbacks that we see—the Black ones—they weren't just the best. They had to do a bunch of other stuff that we didn't see in order to be successful. So, my thing with them, especially the top guys, is helping them navigate not only the on-the-field stuff, but then navigating all the other stuff they have to deal with. They have to deal with coaches being more condescending with them than they are with white counterparts. Things of that nature. I think that's kind of the value that I add. That's the thing that differentiates the most between me dealing with Black quarterbacks versus someone of a different race.

Chad: When you're working and taking fancy meetings, how aware are you of your race?

Quincy: One hundred percent aware. I think about it all the time. When you're a quarterback, you're usually the only Black quarterback. So you know that you gotta have the answers. You also feel like you're doing it for a bunch of other Black quarterbacks all the time. If you don't do this right, they're gonna look at the next Black quarterback a little different. Or, when I go to meeting rooms and I'm asking for sponsorships or whatever, I gotta be a little more buttoned up than whoever it is I'm opposing. Because, I feel they're looking for reasons to not give me the same thing that other guys may have. So that's probably the number one thing I'm thinking about in those meetings.

We also happen to be more aware of the time than everybody else. I'm a young Black man who's kind of gotten to this place in the game and I know that didn't come easily. People don't necessarily wanna see me in the positions that I'm in, so I gotta be more buttoned up. We have to be more on time. Our schedule has to be more together. I found myself telling the biggest training facilities in the country that recently. There's only one of me in the whole country, my age, doing what I'm doing as a young Black man. So, I'm not willing to get someone else even five minutes off their schedule.

Chad: What would you tell younger people who see their race as an impediment, or some kind of force that's going to hold them back in their careers? What would you tell them about how to endure that and how they can find ways to use what they learn from their experiences as Black people to turn things around for themselves?

Quincy: Things that are debilitating can be used as a bonus. It can give you the extra push. There is an advantage in every disadvantage if you just learn how to use it correctly and learn how to push through it and see the good in it. I learned how to communicate with a bunch of people in different ways and use all the things that other people might have used against me. They say dyslexic people might not be great at school, but they end up being great entrepreneurs. You gotta use the thing that others might use against you to benefit in other areas. You have to figure out what it is you're good at and what it is you can do. You have to figure out what it is that your Black skin might help you advance with. Use that and let that be the thing that guides you and allows you to persevere with the things you hope to attain.

I think a lot of people get beaten up or stuck or feel down thinking about the advantages that other people may have because of their skin color. They get white privilege and things of that nature. But there are a lot of advantages to being African-American. We get the advantage of really learning how to persevere at a young age; learning how to communicate. There are so many things that we get the opportunity to do because of our Black skin.

ANDREA TAYLOR LINDSAY

"I married a white guy and I could imagine that our children may be quite fair as well. I want them to never forget that level of heritage and to never forget that they're so lucky to be Black. You have a whole other story to tell that people who aren't Black don't get."

Andrea (Dre) is the cofounder and creative director of Rec Room (rec-room.com), a women's recreation wear company based out of Los Angeles, where Dre grew up. She was formerly a consultant at the Boston Consulting Group, a global brand solutions strategist at YouTube, and an associate in People Operations at Google in California, New York, and London. Dre earned her MBA at Stanford Graduate School of Business and her BA in History at Stanford University.

She and I started at Google on the same day and quickly became friends. It was Dre who, on the day after Trayvon Martin's murderer went free, saw me hiding my sadness and anger and took me to a conference room to stabilize me.

Most people can't tell if Dre is Black when first meeting her. Her skin is very fair. In the sixties and seventies, people might have said she was light enough to pass, meaning she is a Black woman with features resembling those of a white woman. But Dre, as she prefers to be called, didn't try to pass at work or anywhere in her life. I assumed that looking like a white person offered Dre important advantages at work and elsewhere in her life. When we spoke, Dre confirmed that "passing" did open up certain doors. But I was surprised to learn of the insults and racism Dre's skin tone exposed her to. She carried a responsibility to call out and correct racism among white friends and acquaintances who didn't know she was Black.

The experience of feeling othered by white people who thought Dre was white made her want even more to represent Black people. Now, as an entrepreneur, Dre stresses the importance of bringing Black friends with her into places they might otherwise not be welcome. Dre informed me that, historically, Black people have been culture creators and tastemakers, which gives her an advantage in her field—fashion. Dre has been an achiever her entire life, but I admire how she's redefined success for herself. Dre wants her success in life closely tied to the way she defines her Blackness. Her Black Magic is pioneering. Dre has chosen to accept the responsibility of bringing her people along in her professional journey instead of hiding her Blackness to seek safety for herself.

———

Dre: I grew up in Los Angeles. My father grew up in Los Angeles. His father grew up in Los Angeles and his mother grew up in Los Angeles, which is kind of unusual for a family of Black people to have been in Los Angeles that long. It's the only place I've ever called home. Since I left college, I moved every year, apartments or cities. So, LA has always been my place and my heart.

I grew up with a little sister and two parents. My parents are both Black, but both creole Black and look very white, frankly. My dad kind of looks Lebanese, and my mom would get Brazilian in the supermarket, and my sister and I look incredibly different. My sister's quite dark and I'm quite fair. That definitely took its toll on our relationship growing up. We have since become much closer. My parents didn't do the best job of breeding a sense of community or sisterhood between me and my sister until quite late in life. I remember when my mom and I were with my sister, someone stopped us and said, "Oh, your daughters are so beautiful, but they look so different. Do they have the same father?" And my mom had a great reaction, a really quick reaction. "Well, why do you ask?" But really, only externally did my mom give us that community building sense together.

Chad: Dre, you have very fair skin. How has that made your experience unique or uncommon?

Dre: My entire life I've been working to explain to people that I'm Black. When people tell me I'm not full Black, I have to break down the entire American history to them of how I can actually be considered full Black if both of my parents call themselves full Black. I think being fair in Los Angeles was not really, like, a thing. There are a lot of people who look like me in Los Angeles. There are a lot of people who look like me in Louisiana, which is where my mom comes from. It didn't really hit me until college and beyond. I think growing up it was something I was aware of because of my familial context. Like I said, my sister was darker than me.

When I got to college, I started to get this sense that perhaps there was—I'm trying to think of how to say this—an over-sexualization of light-skinned women of any race, really. It was a kind of jarring experience for me both with Black men and with white men. I had only dated white guys in high school, and I got to college and started exploring all the different types of men that I liked. I think being light-skinned definitely affected my love life. I was always wondering if guys liked me because they were doing some kind of fetishizing of light-skinned women—whether light-skinned Hispanic or light-skinned Black. That definitely played a role in how I colored my relationships.

From another perspective, I almost felt protected that I could move pretty freely among different groups of people because of the way that I looked. I was recently in South Africa traveling with a pretty diverse group of people. I was sitting at the pool with a white woman who didn't know that I was Black and I was confused because she was talking about going into a township and how there were all these Black people everywhere and she didn't know what to do. I just looked at her and was like, *Ah, oh my God, you have no clue that I am Black.* I think sometimes I've gotten to access these worlds that I would not have had access to, and in some ways that made me feel kind of privileged. But with that also came a sense of, God, this shit really happens. So many people that are darker colored don't know these types of people. I had to take on that heavy weight of figuring out how to tell that person in South Africa that you can't really say that. How do I communicate that?

I think now that I'm grown up, I'm very, very proud of my heritage and the skills in unpacking how to address that and how to share that out in the world. I'm working on many different art projects to highlight that. One of them is that I'm interviewing women who look like me, who identify as Black by any percentage, but maybe don't look Black to the naked eye. Just writing down these stories came out of a feeling that I needed that. I needed that when I was growing up and I didn't get that.

I married a white guy and I could imagine that our children may be quite fair as well. I want them to never forget that level of heritage and to never forget that they're so lucky to be Black. You have a whole other story to tell that people who aren't Black don't get. I know that sounds kind of crazy, but if you're not Black I almost feel like you don't have this special kernel of history and this special kernel of experience that was given to you. I want to preserve that for my children.

Chad: Why is it special? What's special about it?

Dre: I've been a student of American history forever, as long as I can remember. I majored in it in college and I think the Black American experience is so unique throughout all of history. I think you've never really had this population of people that is mixed from so many different places and backgrounds who have developed into a really incredibly successful and empowered people. I think we're empowered and leave such a big mark on culture.

I think it's always funny that people forget that Black people are only like 13 percent of this country, but they have completely shaped how we look at culture every day. I think it's such a blessing to be a part of that. What a blessing to say you have a role in continuing that notion. However you want to define it, whether you want to be a banker or a musician, you're part of this smaller group of people in a country that has done incredible things and has had awful things in your historical background, but you've persevered. What a story of survival.

To be part of that story of survival is a privilege no matter how you look or how you identify if you're part of this group. I think that's an incredibly powerful thing.

Chad: To make a leap, what about your Black experience or your cultural heritage has been helpful, applicable to your professional journey?

Dre: My family had always instilled in me this belief that you absolutely have to be the best so that no one could say that you got in because you were Black or you got the job because you're Black. You just had to be the best. I was saying earlier that my parents were hard on us and they pushed us really hard to succeed and pushed us hard to do well in school and to go to good colleges. I think they did that because they wanted to make sure we had no excuses. They wanted to make sure we didn't fail and that if we succeeded we could point to our own doing and not have to fight the accusation that we only got in because we were Black.

I think I had a sense of purpose from an early age because I was Black. I got the privilege of sucking up these resources and really channeling it into the best I could be. There was just no doubt in my parents' minds that I had to do something with my career and my family and everything. That was always on my mind.

I found myself gravitating toward programs and mentorships that would celebrate being a Black person in that environment, while also helping me grow. I was in a program at Google called BOLD (Building Opportunities for Leadership Development) that looks to encourage people of color to get involved in tech. I wanted to keep that kernel of community, but also use what I have learned and the experience I knew I had to really drive forward the initiatives I cared about.

I did MLT (Management Leadership for Tomorrow) funded by John Rice, which to some degree came out of my dad's thinking. We had to just make sure that Black candidates had the resources that they need to be the best candidates they can possibly be. That program was absolutely incredible for me and helped me to continue to build that community of people who were Black like me and who wanted to achieve the same success that I wanted to achieve and were willing to support me to get there.

So, I think that what I'm trying to say is that for me, building a career has always come in tandem with building my community and my position in the Black community. It's always been hand in hand. I cannot imagine them unmarried because I think I just looked at the people that had come before me, whether they were in my family or not, and felt like I wanted that.

My grandpa was the first Black deputy superintendent of the LAPD. My great-grandmother founded the first Black Girl Scout troop in LA. I was like, I want that. I want to have my success closely tied to the way I define my Blackness. So, I think that's the type of thing that propelled me in the early days toward current successes and the challenges that I saw in my work life, whether that was at Google or in business school.

Now I'm in apparel. Apparel and beauty and these other consumer spaces are finally starting to get attention from people that care about tapping into this world of color. You see things like Tristan Walker, who is doing everything incredible with Walker & Company that's hyper-tailored to the experience of people of color.

I saw the economic power that people of color wield in this country as tastemakers and I just felt like that was something that I wanted to harness. I wanted to do it for all people. I wanted everyone to have a brand that felt inclusive and diverse and like a seamless part of their life, regardless of how they identified. The way that's manifesting for us now, at Rec Room, is from the outset, we're using diverse models of different body shapes and colors. We're making sure to show how the apparel we make can be used for not just tennis and golf, but going to the grocery store and taking a walk. We want to be a ubiquitous thing that anyone can see themselves using.

Chad: Imagine a young person just starting to engage with her race and the ways her race is going to affect her life and the way she's able to access her dreams. What would you tell her? What kind of advice would you give her before that process begins?

Dre: That's a really good question. I would say, don't let what you think and have been told about your race in your childhood, whether from family or community or strangers, define you in adulthood. Because it really comes down to you. I would say, it's not too late to figure that out for yourself. Here I am: I started really figuring it out for myself in my twenties and I wish I had the confidence to do it earlier. Find people that look like you. I know that sounds corny, but find them and don't even talk to them about looking the same. You just have to find them and exist with them because there will be an unspoken understanding of how to support each other.

Bring people that don't look like you along for the journey because you will always be friends. That's something that you, Chad, said to me when we were at Google. I asked you if it was weird coming from Morehouse into Google and what the transition was like. You said you wished someone had prepared you for the onslaught of non-Black people that were suddenly in your life. I would say the message should be, that is going to be your life for a very long time. Bring your people along. Don't hide from them; bring them along for your journey. Open up to them about your journey. Don't be afraid to share your experience with race and how it's changed and evolved, because they will appreciate that and appreciate your openness.

I believe being a Black woman in America makes you innately ready to work and work hard, to hustle, and the experience primes you for entrepreneurship. There has always been a need in the Black community for women to act as innovative leaders, first for survival, and later as a means to harness creativity. I feel strongly that it's a fantastic and under-sung legacy in the United States—the very first female self-made millionaire in America was a Black woman, Madam C. J. Walker. What an honor to try to follow in those footsteps and be a part of that legacy. I look to her and women like her—Cathy Hughes, Oprah, so many more—as inspiration to keep going with my own brand.

Chapter Five
SPIRIT: CHURCH, GOD, AND FAITH

"What difference do it make if the thing you scared of is real or not?"

—Toni Morrison

When I was six years old my mom taught me how to pray. We had just moved into our single-family home in the suburbs. Its small, square windows looked out on our American Dreamy cul-de-sac, where the other houses in the neighborhood were constructed in the same design, painted in various shades of blue and cream.

My bedroom was painted blue. My parents had placed two wooden dressers on the far wall of my bedroom and two wooden bookshelves on the near wall, close to the door. Together we decorated the ceiling with plastic, stick-on, glow-in-the dark bugs and planets. And to this day they're still hanging on the ceiling, unmoved.

Every night before bed, my mom came into the room with rollers in her hair. I'd be lying in bed, flipping through *Sports Illustrated for Kids*, sounding out tough words phonetically.

I could hear my dad's bursts of belly laughter and my sister's nine-year-old squeaky giggle coming from the next room over. My sister's room was painted pink and *full* of books. She was allowed to stay up thirty minutes longer than me because she was three years older.

One night, I decided it was my turn to lead our nightly prayer.

"Hi Chadster," my mom said. "Time for bed, honey."

As was our ritual, we knelt beside each other, knees on the floor, hands clasped, eyes closed.

"Dear God . . . ," my mom began.

"Mommy, can I say it?" I asked, eyes still closed. The question tickled her. My mom declared often that it was her job to keep our souls safe. That's why she needed to make sure my sister and I had relationships with God.

"If I don't do that, does anything else I do even matter?" she'd say. That job sometimes meant literally dragging my sister and me out of bed at 7 a.m. on Sundays, forcing us into our little Sunday outfits while we protested, crust still in our eyes, and driving us to the People's Community Baptist Church on New Hampshire road. The People's Community Baptist Church was big, Black, and loud. Every Sunday Pastor Baltimore led us in examining the previous week's victories and tragedies. We celebrated Honor Roll students and college graduates and anniversaries and newborns together. We held each other and sang together and swayed and prayed our way through the months and years. Every week People's gave us confidence and hope and strength to face whiteness at work and school. There was a life-or-death fastidiousness to the way people clung to that church. People's was a fill-up station for thousands of Black folks in our pocket of Maryland. At the end of each service Pastor Baltimore announced that the doors of the church were open, and fifteen visitors would make their way to the front of the pulpit to join us, some in tears. Those Black people decided they needed God and they needed a place to be with others who needed God.

I never thought deeply about why we went to church and prayed. It was just what we did, the way some families go to the movies or the pool on weekends. We went to church. We went every Sunday. There was little my sister and I could do to weasel out of it. Pretending to be sick could get me out of school, but I attended many a Sunday church service drowsy on Children's Robitussin. God was unavoidable in our house.

So on this night, my mom must have felt some validation when I asked to say the prayer.

"Sure, sweetie. Go ahead," she encouraged.

"Dear God," I began. "Please help my parents buy me Super Nintendo for my birthday. In Jesus' name we pray. Amen."

"Amen," my mom repeated. Then she started to laugh. I opened my eyes. I was confused. Did I do it wrong?

"Chadster, remember to thank God first when you pray and *then* ask for what you want," she instructed. She squeezed my nose playfully, but I knew she was serious. "It's important to be grateful before you ask God for more."

I took the message to heart as I grew. Every night, my parents led our family in prayer over our food. And then we prayed again before bed. We prayed for strength and purpose and hope. We prayed for safety. My parents prayed that when they sent my sister and me out into the world that we would return.

I continued to pray at bedside every night in college in Atlanta, first thanking God for what I had, then asking for what I wanted. I knelt every night in prayer when I moved to Oakland and felt alone and defeated at Google. I thanked God for opportunity. I prayed for confidence and to feel like myself again. When I left the tech industry for show business, I knelt every night in prayer. I thanked God for health and family and independence. I prayed for the courage to drown out my fear of failure. I prayed for money to find me. I prayed that I wasn't ruining my life. Every night, wherever I was sleeping, I sank to my knees to thank God and ask for help. Sometimes, I'd wake up after big nights out at 4 or 5 a.m., kneeling on the side of the bed with the lights and TV on, fully clothed and a burning pizza in the oven. The instinct to pray became muscle memory.

In the summer of 2015, when Brett and I were still friends, before he broke our trust by using the n-word, we watched a UFC match in his parents' opulent Tribeca condo. His family was in Millburn, New Jersey, where they lived on the estate where Brett grew up. I was never invited there. Brett warned that his parents were not as racially sensitive as he was. But I was often at their place in the city, and I wondered if they'd walk in the door unexpectedly one day and tell me to leave. That day, I stared out the floor-to-ceiling windows, facing the Hudson River. All three of the bedrooms were larger than any I'd seen in Manhattan or Brooklyn.

Brett was a mixed martial arts fanatic and this was, apparently, a very important match. Brett's eyes were glued to the undercard fights on the seventy-two-inch TV screen. On commercial breaks, he played chess against himself on the crystal chess board sitting atop the bar on the far wall of the living room. I sat on the black leather couch beneath a Basquiat painting scrolling my phone, looking up at the fights only when the crowd shrieked. I never had a stomach for the violence of MMA. But Brett was obsessed with MMA fighting and this was a match he had circled on the calendar months ago.

When I looked up at the screen, I saw two 170-pound Black men fighting in the caged Octagon. One was American and the other Brazilian. They were trim and focused and beating on each other ruthlessly. We watched in silence for thirty seconds while the American pinned the Brazilian man to the mat, using only his left forearm. Then the American raised his right hand high above his head. He closed it into a fist and bashed the Brazilian's face until it bled. The crowd, comprised mostly of middle-aged white men, cheered. Brett watched, entranced. The Brazilian stopped struggling. He was unconscious. The referee grabbed the American in a bear hug and pulled him away from his senseless and bleeding opponent.

The American fighter stood up and flexed his muscles. He roared. Sweat and blood dripped down over his bulging muscles and dark, ebony skin. Then he dropped to his knees, clenched his hands in prayer, and closed his eyes. He mumbled a few words under his breath and then sprang back to his feet. He pointed up to the ceiling. He smiled. The crowd outside the caged Octagon whooped and cheered. They gave the American a standing ovation for his bloody victory.

I wondered what the fighter said to God when he knelt on his knees. Had he remembered to thank him first? Had he thanked him for keeping him alive through another fight, his twenty-fourth as a professional? And then what did he ask God for? Another man to destroy? A check big enough to buy his way out of the game?

Brett was still glued to the screen. I bet he wasn't thinking about God.

And I was confused by the cheers from the crowd. I wondered if these middle-aged white men, and Brett, were cheering for the American, as an athlete and a competitor, or if they were cheering for the brutal beat-down he'd levied on a guy who looked like he could have been his brother. The post-fight interview began, but the fighter grabbed the interviewer's microphone before any questions were asked.

"Thank you, Jesus Christ, my lord and savior who strengthens me!" the fighter yelled into the microphone. He was still dripping blood and sweat. Brett had stopped paying attention and resumed his chess match against himself. He was looking down at the board.

"Do you ever think about why God put us here instead of in there?" I asked him. A God shot of the caged UFC Octagon showed its floor stained with blood. Brett looked up at me over his chessboard. He muted the TV.

"I *strongly* don't believe in God," he said. There was a trace of a smirk on his face. I wasn't surprised. During my time working in technology a few software engineers went out of their way to tell me they were atheists. Sometimes they announced it out of nowhere. Once it happened after I'd said a quick prayer to bless my food in the cafeteria. It felt like they wanted me to spar with them about my beliefs. I recognized that in Brett now. I had never taken the bait before, but Brett was a friend, so I engaged.

"I do," I said. Brett didn't say anything for a while. The room was completely quiet now with the TV muted.

Then he asked: "Why do so many Black people believe in God?" He continued: "Why would you believe in a God who would do *this* to you?" Brett was a well-intentioned, rich liberal. We discussed race politics often. By this point we were close enough friends to have developed a shorthand. I knew that by *this* he was referring to the brutalized and marginalized state of Black people.

I could still see the Black fighter on screen, glistening with blood and sweat. But Brett's gaze was now fixed on me.

From him, the question threw me. But I was surprised how quickly an answer found me.

"We probably need God more." What I meant was that God gives us hope we often can't find in the world. On the screen were two Black men fighting each other for prize money. What I meant was God helps me believe we'll get to live in mansions in Jersey and have weekend apartments in Tribeca instead of fighting for drunken crowds. And while some people dream of fighting in the arena, and spend their entire lives training toward that end, I thought maybe they'd have other dreams that didn't require them to sacrifice their bodies had they been born another color.

Brett didn't ask any follow-up questions. He just turned back to his chess game, chewing on what I had said. I looked back out those floor-to-ceiling windows.

Why do Black people believe in God? I'd considered the question on my own many times before. In grade school when I learned about slavery, mass incarceration, government-sponsored experimentation on Black people, and police brutality, I'd considered the question. Why would Black Americans believe in a God who built a world that tried to hold us on the mat and beat us unconscious? And yet, we are the demographic with the most absolute certainty in his existence. According to the PEW Research Center on Religion and Public Life, 97 percent of us believe in God.[*]

Maybe we need to believe that a treacherous life here on earth isn't all we have to look forward to. Maybe just to get out of bed in the morning, we need to believe in heaven, an afterlife, a spiritual existence with our loved ones without teenage girls stabbing each other in high school parking lots and routine traffic stops that turn into executions and fathers tied to train tracks. Maybe faith is our last resort.

I learned to pray to God as a child, but I learned to believe in the Spirit as a teenager. There was one other non-white student in most of my classes from preschool through high school: Alicia Betancourt. She was Puerto Rican. She was a lifeline for me. We retreated together to the back of classrooms when racial tension flared. Like in Advanced Placement History, when our teacher, Mr. Dickau, went on a rant decrying Malcolm X's aggressive civil rights tactics. Mr. Dickau kept saying that violent resistance was a tool of less intelligent leaders. That stung me. I found his analysis of a Black legend reductive. Malcolm X was a man with flaws, but unintelligent? That was a baseless insult.

"You take a more educated, thoughtful leader like Dr. Martin

---

[*] PEW Research Center—Religion and Public Life, https://www.pewforum .org/religious-landscape-study/belief-in-god/.

Luther King, Jr., and it's clear that he had a deeper understanding of how to affect change and move people," Mr. Dickau said.

"That sounds like an opinion," I blurted out.

"Excuse me," he said.

"I said that sounds like an opinion," I repeated. "It's not your job to spew opinions. Your job is to teach facts."

I sat up taller in my seat. Mr. Dickau's icy blue eyes narrowed.

"Do you want to come up here and teach the class?" he asked. Classmates who were dozing off paid attention now. I felt Alicia's hand on mine. I clenched my jaw. I had been waiting for my moment to joust with Mr. Dickau for a long time.

"They can't afford me on your salary," I fired back. It was an ugly, low blow. And Mr. Dickau snapped.

"Get the hell out of my classroom!" he said.

I marched out with a smile on my face and slammed the door behind me. I reached my locker and sat down beside it. I had left my books and backpack in the classroom. I folded my arms and stared at the floor. I was just going to wait there until the next period.

Until I saw Alicia. She walked around the corner toward me in the empty hallway. She was petite, five-foot-one and slight—but carrying my heavy backpack full of books and hers too. She smiled. She knew from how I felt, and how long I had held my tongue when my teachers like Mr. Dickau promoted prejudiced opinions instead of facts. But as she sat down beside me, she still asked the question.

"What was that?" She was amused. She had known me since I was six years old. She thought it was funny when I tried to bare teeth. She knew I was just a nice, suburban kid who wet the bed until he was twelve and still used a night-light at sixteen. She wasn't buying my door-slamming performance.

"You know, we need to pass Dickau to graduate," she said.

"Yeah," I muttered.

"He can be a pig," she said. "But we just have to do the work and get through the class. You need to accept that."

I knew she was right. And I knew she was on my team. Alicia wasn't Black, but she felt micro-aggressed, silenced, isolated, and invisible in all her own ways through all of our mostly white classes. She said classmates used racial epithets to describe people of Latin heritage around her; she had neighbors who didn't want to share space with her family.

But Alicia had perspective to remind me that we needed to get through Dickau to move forward. And that meant we needed to accept his authority. I had to swallow my disappointment and sadness and anger to get to graduation. There was no way around that.

Alicia walked out in the middle of Dickau's lesson to tell me that I should return and apologize—because she knew that if I didn't I might suffer a failing grade or expulsion, which could derail my path to graduation and college. She was telling me to protect myself, and the only way to do that was to bend over.

It was so unlike Alicia to walk out of a class. I felt grateful. And then I felt selfish. I realized that when I left that classroom I'd left her alone in there. She and I had been each other's lifeline in those tense classrooms for over a decade.

I returned to class and apologized to Dickau. He accepted my apology with smug arrogance and reassured me that I was a *good kid*. I felt ashamed for apologizing then and the feeling remains just as strong today. But, like Alicia said, I had to get through Dickau.

I promised Alicia I wouldn't leave her in class like that again.

◆ ◆

A few months later, early in the morning, I was asleep in my twin bed when my family's cordless phone rang. I grabbed the big black phone and pushed the accept button.

"Hello?" I said, groggy.

"Chad . . ." It was my ex-girlfriend. I was surprised to hear from her. We talked on the phone often, but she never called so early on a weekend. Her voice cracked.

"Hey, what time is it?" I asked.

"Hey Chad." She sounded so . . . off. She kept repeating my name.

"Alicia was in a car accident last night."

I got up to put my clothes on. I looked for my keys to the Hearse. All my friends were new drivers at that age. I figured Alicia had gotten into a fender bender and maybe cracked a wrist.

"Damn, where is she? Do her parents know? I'll go see her right now."

"You're not listening, Chad. She's gone."

I've heard people talk about the wave of grief that unmoored them when they lost someone close. I didn't feel that. I felt dry, and stuck. I felt such empty certainty. I felt like I got older in a moment—I knew something concrete about my future, that Alicia would not be in it.

I think I thanked my ex for the call and returned the phone to its charging port in my parents' room. I walked out of the house. It was a Saturday. The neighborhood was sunny and quiet. The cars were in their garages. Nobody was walking dogs on the street or pushing strollers down the sidewalks. I walked alone through our neighborhood, wearing the clothes I had slept in. I strolled for half an hour or so, up and down each cul-de-sac, around the streets that twisted through the townhouses further in our neighborhood. There was nothing to do. Everything was quiet. After that call, I began taking long walks every single day. I just walk in silence, sometimes talking to myself or God or Alicia.

Alicia had been in the passenger seat of a small car when the teenage driver sped off the wet road and slammed into a telephone pole two blocks from our high school. The driver was in a coma for weeks, but survived. Alicia died instantly.

I started talking to Alicia sometimes when I knelt bedside to say my prayers each night. I asked God to keep her spirit close to me. And she felt close. Maybe closer than ever. Previously, when I wanted to talk to her, I had to call her on the phone, or drive my old Volvo fifteen minutes to her neighborhood and wait for her to answer the door in her pajamas. Now all I had to do was get still and focus on her voice and hear what her spirit was saying to mine. I felt like I could talk to my friend through prayer. Brett and my atheist coworkers would probably call that rationalizing. They'd say that when I was praying, I was just thinking, meditating, talking to myself. They'd say my parents taught me to believe in God to give me hope in a hopeless world, so that when I lost someone—like I lost Alicia—I would still feel like I could reach her, all so I wouldn't be depressed. They'd say I was being weak and illogical. They'd say I was believing in fairy tales. But it made me feel better.

I missed Alicia especially in my senior year of high school. I was exhausted from twelve years of racial isolation, and now without her as a lifeline. I gave up on defending my point of view in class discussions. I sunk deeper into my seat in the back of my classrooms. I stopped participating. I felt unsafe. If I called attention to myself in some way, if I took on a classmate or a teacher, I knew nobody would come find me in the hallway afterward. I just needed to get through. Get to the buzzer. Get to my Black basketball teammates in the hallway. Get to Coach Pigrom. Get to my parents and sister.

The year Alicia died was the same year I witnessed the murder of the teenage girl in the green hoodie in the parking lot after that football game. Both deaths occurred on the same street as my presumably safe, suburban high school. I saw the imminent danger in the world for the first time. That danger is what my parents had tried to protect me from my whole life. I realized my parents—and their rules—couldn't protect me. No one could. And yet I had to go to school and learn. I had to enter the workforce and earn. I had a responsibility to myself, and my family and all Black people to achieve so that we might have any chance to undo our treacherous circumstances.

❖ ❖

It is easy for us as Black people to tell ourselves bleak stories about our futures. We can reach for any number of available statistics. One in three Black men will go to prison. More than half of all 2017 murder arrests in the United States were Black. Black people make up 13 percent of the US population, but 31 percent of people in the US killed by police. And if we ever lack data, we can turn to the news, social media, comedy, music,

Ta-Nehisi Coates's *Between the World and Me*, or the Oscar-nominated movies each year for a depiction of our hopelessness. Black Twitter offers an endless loop of news reports about police brutality, wrongful incrimination, and Black-on-Black violence. Even contemporary masterpieces by Black directors focus on our trapped existences both when surrounded by Blackness—as in Barry Jenkins's hood elegy *Moonlight*—and when surrounded by whiteness—as in Jordan Peele's incisive exposé of white liberals *Get Out* (my favorite movie). Just last August one of my high school teammates, Adam Fongyen, was shot and killed in front of his house in Washington, DC, an incident that leaves his three-year-old son to grow up fatherless. We can choose any reason to be hopeless, and find confirmation of that hopelessness.

And yet so many Black folks believe in the unseen. So many of us choose faith. Remember: 97 percent according to the researchers. Hardheaded faith is expressed in many forms, even outside of church: hissing defiance (think Kendrick Lamar), powerful confidence (think President Barack Obama), bold pioneering (think Oprah Winfrey), unbridled free expression (think Prince, Beyoncé, André 3000, Erykah Badu). Many of us choose to believe we've already beaten the odds just by enjoying our lives, by being happy. Our ancestors survived the Middle Passage and more than five hundred years of violent physical and psychological attacks, both overt and disguised. Our existence defies logic. The odds have been against us and yet, somehow, our president *was* Black.

Faced with the statistical case against our happiness and success, many of us tap into the *unreal* for permission to exist. *God.* The Universe. Our ancestors. The spirits of our friends and family members, dead too soon and unfairly. We tap into these sources because the other option is to be paralyzed by hopelessness. As a teenager I saw the violence and loneliness that exists in the world and chose faith. I went where the love was. The other option was no option.

The faith we have forged through suffering and surviving as Black people strengthens us. It's a desperate faith. It's a back-against-the-wall faith. That faith is *Black Magic*. And every entrepreneur and business leader needs faith to believe and inspire others to believe in a vision yet to be realized.

PASTOR ROGER JAMISON

"I hated religion, man. I hated religion. I believed that religion was an opiate of the masses. And I believed it was how white folks indoctrinated us."

Pastor Jamison is the senior pastor at Sword of the Spirit Tabernacle in Bed Stuy, Brooklyn. He began his career in the Rikers Island Correctional Facility more than forty years ago and still ministers there. He recently retired as program director for Anchor House, a residential program for recovering substance users, where Pastor Jamison served for over twenty years. He continues to provide counsel to clients and staff at Anchor House on a volunteer basis.

There's a rugged quality about Pastor Jamison. He has a broad neck and shoulders. His eye contact pierces. At close to seventy years old, his strong body still denotes the powerful frame of a college basketball player. He speaks directly to, and never over, his congregation of thirty or so Black Brooklynites every Sunday morning. There are no fancy bells and whistles in his church to lure God seekers. No sexy welcome video or five-piece band playing melodies throughout service. Just a few dozen worshipers, taking the bus and subway to connect with God and each other for a two-hour-long service, where Pastor Jamison connects scriptures to the troubling world we live in today. It's where I go to be with people. It's where I go for a fill-up on love and affirmation.

I'm reminded of what drew me into Pastor Jamison's congregation when I interviewed him for this book. He is blunt, honest, and vulnerable. Roger Jamison was a suicidal drug addict who robbed and sold drugs, then became a pastor and father figure to prisoners and at-risk young people all over New York.

Pastor Jamison stands so steady in his sense of racial pride today. He sent all three of his children to HBCUs for college. So I was shocked to learn that at one point he resented his own Blackness so much that he contemplated suicide. His rage against racism boiled so hot that he even cursed out legendary UNC basketball coach Dean Smith.

Pastor Jamison just barely survived his young adulthood. He eventually devoted his life to ministering to the most down-and-out Black people in New York City. He believes Black Magic exists in our closeness and access to God. But why should we have such special access? Pastor Jamison believes the reason is our desperation. We believe because we're desperate. Where the tangible world has given us pain and dead ends, we have turned to the supernatural.

———

Roger: To be honest with you, man, growing up I didn't believe in God.

Chad: How did you grow up?

Roger: I was born in 1951, so when I was eleven years old is when Martin Luther King had a civil rights march in Greensboro, North Carolina, where I lived. Growing up in the Jim Crow South, I remember riding in the back of the bus. I remember drinking from Black fountains. I was nine, ten, eleven years old then.

I came out of a very abusive family where my father was schizophrenic when we knew nothing about what that term meant. He was physically abusive up to the point of pulling out weapons. I had an experience with my dad at four years old when I had pneumonia. I woke up in his bed. He pulled out a snub-nose, .32-caliber, pearl-handle revolver and put it between my eyes and said he would blow my brains out.

There were times I'd be eating breakfast, watching *Mighty Mouse* on TV and he would come in and pull out two rifles and shoot them off in the air while we were sitting there in the kitchen.

Chad: How did that sort of environment change you?

Roger: There was so much racism, segregation, discrimination where I grew up. The impact of that on me was so major, and it didn't come from interacting with white people, it came from interacting with Black people. I didn't really deal with white people until I was fifteen years old. But amongst Black folks there was such classism. The mentality was "If you're white, you're right, if you're brown you can stick around, but if you're Black you got to get back." I had such a self-hatred of my own skin color. I hated myself. I hated that I was put in this Black skin. I remember crying myself to sleep because I would wake up and I was still Black. I mean dark-skinned Black.

This mentality was deeply entrenched in the sixties. It was horrible. I had to deal with being called Mighty Joe Young and King Kong from Black people, not from white people, from Black people.

Chad: What did that do to you?

Roger: My self-esteem and self-worth, internally, was nothing. I remember going to pick up a young lady for a high school dance. She was very light-skinned with freckles. I show up to pick her up and there's a brown bag next to the door [for her mom to measure against my skintone]. Her mom comes out— her mom looks white. And she said, "Can I help you? You're not going anywhere with my daughter. You're just too Black."

My only saving grace as a child was that I was a voracious reader. I basically grew up in Carnegie Library at Bennett College in Greensboro. In the eighth grade I began to play basketball and became one of the best junior high school players. I went to high school and started every game from my sophomore year to my senior year. I was a straight-A student and I found out a lot of my success came because I grew up in such a dysfunctional family. My dad was the addict. My mom was an enabler and then all the kids took on various roles. I became the mascot. I was scholarly and athletic but struggling with my own Blackness.

From high school, where there were only a couple hundred Blacks, I went to a junior college on a full basketball scholarship, where there were twenty-five Blacks. There were only three Black women and the rest were Black athletes. It was in the Blue Ridge Mountains. People would tell us that if you were Black you don't want to be outside when the sun goes down. That was the 1970s.

One day I got a call from Dean Smith, the head basketball coach at University of North Carolina. He said, "I don't have any scholarships but I'll offer you a walk-on position." I went to Carolina and beat four guys out for a full scholarship. At that time, I was all about performance and approval. On the inside, there was still self-hatred, but I was able to mask it through sports.

I was the fifth African-American to play for Dean Smith. I was the token Black on the bench, and so I was still being shaped by this Jim Crow racist situation. I was better than his point guards, but because their parents were alumni I didn't get to play. I ended up cursing Dean Smith out and I quit the team. I called him a racist dog. Leaving basketball left such a void in me. Up until this point, ball really played a big part in maintaining my whole balance. I began to fill that void with drugs.

Chad: What kind of drugs?

Roger: Alcohol, marijuana. At one point I would have a pound of marijuana in my possession at all times. I was high every day, all day for three months after I quit the team. I was then introduced to acid, LSD. I had such a void. Up until that point, my God was basketball.

Chad: Did drugs become your God?

Roger: Yeah, they became my escape. I was an extremist, so you know, there was no social drinking for me. It was zero to one hundred. And so I went from being on scholarship to flunking out of school. I became very, very depressed. Self-hatred really overwhelmed me. I began to have the first ideation of suicide. I considered taking my own life. The basketball dorm at UNC was a high-rise hotel. I was up on the tenth floor and I remember smoking in my depression, and as I'm smoking I just had this thought that I need to just end all of this. Just jump. And it was a real force. At this point I had no father, no one to help me. No one in my family had ever gotten a high school diploma. All my emotional stuff and feelings of self-hatred and low self-esteem and low self-worth and all this stuff coming from the affliction of being born Black and poor really hit me.

I went back to Greensboro and continued with the drinking and drugging and still dealing with the racism. I could only get labor jobs until a friend recommended me for a government job as an account specialist taking inventory of city property. I walked into the interview and there were two white guys there. They sat me down and looked at my résumé and said, "You know, you're overqualified for this job." I said yeah, but I need to work. One of the guys said, "Listen, I would rather send this money back to the government before I hire you." He said it with a straight face.

Chad: That's hopeless.

Roger: Come on brother! Chad, man, I went back home and cried, bruh. I cried, I cried, I cried. I cried like a baby. I just cried. I said, wow. I just cried. And I said, okay. I can't get it legally or legitimately. I'll get it with a gun.

But right before I went down that road I got a job at a hospital as a pharmacist's technician.

I had all the oxycodone, all the Percocet, whatever I wanted. I was still getting high and I began to steal drugs from the hospital and sell them. I stole a five-gallon jar of something called procaine hydrochloride. I sold it all over North Carolina to the colleges. I sold it as cocaine, Chad, but it wasn't coke. Procaine hydrochloride is basically anesthesia. It freezes you up. Numbs you up. But Southern people didn't know it wasn't coke. I stole a five-gallon jar of something called phenobarbital. It's like sleeping pills. And it was dangerous.

Well my boy, Deacon, overdosed on the phenobarbital and it took him into a coma for two weeks. His family didn't think he was gonna make it. I went home and flushed all that stuff down the toilet and said: God if you save my friend, I'll never do this again. It was one of those foxhole prayers.

Chad: Why did you pray to God at that moment when you said you weren't a believer this whole time?

Roger: I wasn't a believer. In fact, during this time I searched and studied Eastern mysticism. I studied mysticism, voodoo-ology. In fact the crimes that I was committing in the hospital, I was using witchcraft to do these things.

Chad: What do you mean?

Roger: I mean I began to conjure up forces that would make me invisible. In most of these crimes where I stole these drugs, I stole them in broad daylight. I'd walk in and walk out and not be seen. And I believed that it was the forces of darkness. But now I'm twenty-three and my friend is in a coma, dying. And I cried out to God and said: "If you save my friend, I'll never do this again." And I flushed the drugs. Well, Deacon came out of that coma.

Chad: And did that make you a believer?

Roger: Nah, bruh. I got worse. Two weeks after he got out of the hospital, a friend of ours brought us an idea. There was a tavern in the outskirts of town where white men would gather to gamble. So we prepared to rob this place. Me and three other of my friends. On Halloween, 1975, we dressed in black on black on black in the woods, like a shadow. We went in there and there were over fifty men inside. We took everything they had. We realized that they were police and firemen. We left them standing in the middle of the floor with no clothes on. I had a .357, my friend had a M16, and another friend had a .32.

We robbed these guys and while we were waiting for the getaway car, on a dark country road in the sticks in North Carolina, a highway patrolman pulled up right across the street from us. They must have had a silent alarm or something. My gun was cocked. He got out of the car and didn't see us. He looked around, got back in his car, and drove away. At that moment I was ready to shoot him, man. I was ready to take his life. And I had two other guys with guns too. Any one of us could have shot the guy.

He got in the car and drove off. We got in the car and got away.

And that opened up doors where I began to follow Black businessmen and prepare to rob them and all kinds of crazy stuff. I hooked up with this guy who was a heroin addict who was really demonic and really lost. One morning after a night of bingeing, we went to the largest church in my hometown. We walked down the middle of the aisle in front of over fifteen hundred people who all knew and recognized me. We walked right up to the front and cursed the preacher out. Nobody walked toward us, no ushers, nobody.

Chad: Why?

Roger: What do you mean why? I hated religion, man. I hated religion. I believed that religion was an opiate of the masses. And I believed it was how white folks indoctrinated us. It was a panacea they used to placate us. I was really a lost soul. I had really lost my way. No dad.

So when my friend Deacon said he was going up to New York to get away from Greensboro, I said, "I need to go with you." I had never been to New York in my life. At twenty-five, I got a one-way ticket, didn't know a soul. Me and Deacon would get high and take acid and LSD and read the Bible out loud to each other and just trip.

Chad: Where does that come from?

Roger: I think it was the calling of God in my life. I think that God's hand had been on me and I always had a hunger for the supernatural. That was me, man. I would say: "Lord please help me get myself together."

Chad: So you were always looking for somebody to save you?

Roger: I was looking for relevance. I felt I was too intelligent to be religious. Because I had questions. I could not embrace religion. I'll be honest with you, I'm not a religious person today. I really despise religion.

Chad: Why do our people believe?

Roger: So, check this out. And I'll never forget these dates. It was November 17, 1976. Deacon goes on a date with this girl and while on the date with her they have a supernatural encounter with Jesus Christ. Deacon and his date come over to my apartment in Queens, at maybe 1 or 2 a.m. I let them in. They come in so lit up, I mean bright, *lit up*, and I say: "Yo, Deacon, whatever that is, bro, I gotta get some of that." And the woman that he was with came from behind him and said, "What you see here, is Jesus." Well, Chad. It's been over thirty years since that happened. Deacon's date that night became my wife.

After that night, I began to stop using drugs. I had a terrible nicotine addiction. I smoked two to three packs per day. Couldn't stop. Hated it. Wanted to stop but I was just too addicted. By December I stopped getting high, but I was still struggling with suicidal ideations. I remember New Year's Eve 1975. I was apartment A17, at 112-22 East 37th Avenue in Corona, Queens. I felt like I didn't want to live. I had really decided to take my life. It was dark, I had candles on, I'm in the lotus position, and I found a scripture because I wanted to finally touch God. I'm chanting "Seek ye first the kingdom of God and his righteousness and all these things shall be added unto you."

I got so frustrated because I wasn't feeling anything. I wanted my life to end. I cried out. I said, "God, if you are real, if you made me, if you created the stars, the moon, and the sky, and if you made me, why can't you talk to me? Lord if you reveal yourself to me, I'll serve you for the rest of my life." And Chad, at that moment, I'm telling you bro, at that moment I broke down. At that moment I literally heard a voice. I heard a voice. I'm by myself in this apartment, I heard a voice. And the voice said, "I am the Holy spirit! I will dry your tears! Stand up and rejoice!"

And brother when I stood up, I felt like shackles were falling off of me. At twenty-six years old I broke down in tears. I knew I had been saved. I knew I was born again. God changed my nature. I cried out because I hated cigarettes. I begged him to take them away from me. And that's the last time I ever had a cigarette to my mouth, brother. It's been forty-five years.

Chad: And let me ask you this—it sounds like you had a very tough journey to this place where you literally cried out to Jesus. Why do Black folks turn there? You've worked with Black prisoners, drug addicts, orphans, all kinds of people trying to cope. What is it that makes people turn to God when they reach the end of their rope?

Roger: Power. That's the thing. I needed power to change. The first thing I realized was that my addiction to nicotine just disappeared. You gotta understand, I'm smoking three packs of cigarettes every day. Real addiction. That's real. I went from that to being repulsed by the smell of cigarettes.

Desperation. Listen, man. What is it that makes us turn to Christ? I believe it's more than the oppressor giving us his God. Christ came for the oppressed, for the broken. He came for the oppressed. And that's where we come in.

Chad: So then do we have special access to him because of that?

Roger: I believe so.

Chad: What can we do with that?

Roger: When Christ was carrying the cross and it was too much for him to carry, the Roman soldiers chose a Black man to help Christ carry his cross to Calvary.

Chad: So what does that mean for us? What does that mean for us?

Roger: Well, I believe that it means that because we carry this gospel, we carry Christ like nobody else does. We're spirit people. That's why very seldom did you ever meet a Black atheist.

Chad: Is that just in our nature?

Roger: We're spirit people, brother. We're spirit people. That's why we dance. It shows in our art. It shows in our dance. It's spirit, brother. Spirit. With passion. We're spirit people, bro. It's who he made us. When I embrace Christ, I embrace my purpose. I never embraced religion. I still don't embrace religion. Christ never came to make us religious. Christ came to make us Children of God.

Chad: What must we do to access our connection to God as Black people? In a moment of desperation or need, how do we access that connection?

Roger: What things you desire when you pray, believe you will receive them. Mine came out of desperation. And I've come to realize that God answers the prayers of desperate people. I'd rather be in a room of inmates and criminals than a room of preachers. Because they're desperate. Give me a room of brothas, because brothas are desperate.

BELIEVE IT OR NOT

"The moment you doubt whether you can fly, you cease
forever to be able to do it."

—J. M. Barrie, *Peter Pan*

◆◆◆◆◆

This is not a book about God or religion, and I don't care
whether or not you believe in either. This is a book about belief. The moment we cease to believe—not in God, or religion,
or spirits, or heritage—but in the very tangible and useful skills
we have learned from suffering since slavery, then we are hopeless. When we stop believing that we have inside us the ability
to transcend our painful circumstance, then we're truly dead
in our tracks. I have worked with and read dozens of books
by and about exceptional leaders and entrepreneurs. In them,
nearly all of the leaders point first to the belief that they could
achieve their vision as the core element in moving themselves
and the people around them toward that goal. After all, Dr.
Martin Luther King, Jr., didn't say "I have a market advantage"
or "I have venture capital funding," he said he had a dream. A
dream, even a glimmer of hope, just enough to hang on to, is
enough for me to keep going. If I believe this world is hopeless

for Black people, then I will quit trying to be happy and I will quit trying to self-actualize. If I believe that Black Magic does not exist, then the brutal and ubiquitous force of racism is insurmountable, and my dreams are unattainable.

But I believe that my ancestors, my parents, and now I, myself, have adapted a set of tools and tactics through suffering that we can use to prosper. If I believe surviving Blackness in this world allows me to summon certain abilities—presence of mind, empathy, independent thinking, conviction, comfort in isolation, work ethic, resourcefulness, bravery, focus, leadership, perseverance, community, detachment, charisma, problem solving, and faith—then I have Black Magic. And if I have Black Magic then I have hope.

◆ ◆

If.

Acknowledgments

I acknowledge my family, which gives me strength and extends well beyond blood relatives. You know who you are.

I thank God, who works in mysterious ways, for the gift of voice.

I gratefully acknowledge everyone who made time to offer me their experiences for this book. In this space, I especially thank those who gave me testimonies that did not make it into the book. You were not quoted, but your spirits are felt in this work. I'll mention a few by name, but there were many others: Sydney Morton, Ashley Lamothe, Ebony Pope, Kyle Mosley, Leon Chitman.

Thank you Coach Damon Pigrom and Coach Marcus Wiggins for being young, Black role models in my teenage years when I needed you most. Thank you Brother Henry Goodgame for guiding me through college and beyond.

Thank you Oronde Garrett, my brother, for believing in me without anyone else's cosign.

Thank you Angie Martinez for opening your doors like family.

Thank you Spike Lee for pushing me to accept myself as an artist.

Thank you Will Packer for being a brother, a partner and a role model.

Thank you Morgan Freeman for believing in my gift.

Thank you Terrence Jenkins for believing in my creativity before I had anyone else's attention.

Thank you Tom Straw for sharing your mastery of the craft with me.

Thank you Elaine Welteroth for showing me how to get in the game.

Thank you Dr. John Wilson for making an introduction that changed my life.

Thank you Tina Wells for making an introduction that changed my life.

Thank you Kenya Barris for my first experience in a writers' room.

Thank you to everyone who contributed to the creation and production of this book:

Emily Graff, my editor.

Eve Attermann, my agent.

Lashanda Anakwah.

Cat Boyd.

Franchesca Carlos.

Jason Hodes.

Jay Mandel.

Thank you LaFawn Bailey for seeing something in me as a college senior. You showed me a bigger world.

Thank you Jamila Lyn and Sarah Mahoney who nurtured me as a young writer.

Thank you Dr. Arturo Betancourt and Lulu Delacre for being family to me.

Thank you Aunt Teree, Aunt Delores, Uncle Jeff, and Uncle Emmanuel for being family to me.

Thank you Uncle Bill and Uncle Mason for showing me my first dream job.

Thank you to the Woodshed and the Humbles.

Thank you to A-Rho. Thank you to the X.

Thank you to Morehouse College.

Thank you Troop 96.

Thanks to anyone who let me crash on a couch, floor, or air mattress when that was exactly what I needed. Thank you Justin and Taylor Lovett. Thank you Leon and Kristin Chitman. Thank you Kyle and Davlyn Mosley. Thank you Elaine and Jonathan. Thank you Jason. Thank you Ed.

Thank you to everyone who makes LA feel like a second home. Thank you Chris, Vanessa, Chris and Bella Spencer. Thank you Y'lan Taylor. Thank you Donald Isaac. Thank you Kristin Valentine. Thank you Andy Allo. Thank you Shayla Cowan. Thank you Emily Smith. Thank you Shion Takeuchi.

Thank you to the companies who gave me canvas space on their platforms:

Simon & Schuster.

The New York Times.

Universal Pictures.

Peacock.

Freeform.

BET.

Slam magazine.

Teen Vogue.

40 Acres and a Mule Filmworks.

Will Packer Productions.

Revelations Entertainment.

To anyone I've left out, and there are many, I'm grateful for you.

And again, thank you God.